THOMAS MANN

BOOKS BY THOMAS MANN

Fiction (now in print)

THE BELOVED RETURNS (*Lotte in Weimar*)
BUDDENBROOKS
THE BLACK SWAN
CONFESSIONS OF FELIX KRULL, CONFIDENCE MAN
THE HOLY SINNER
DOCTOR FAUSTUS
JOSEPH AND HIS BROTHERS
   THE TALES OF JACOB
   YOUNG JOSEPH
   JOSEPH IN EGYPT
   JOSEPH THE PROVIDER
THE MAGIC MOUNTAIN
ROYAL HIGHNESS
STORIES OF THREE DECADES
THE TABLES OF THE LAW
THE TRANSPOSED HEADS

Non-Fiction

ESSAYS OF THREE DECADES
LAST ESSAYS
A SKETCH OF MY LIFE
THE STORY OF A NOVEL: THE GENESIS OF DOCTOR FAUSTUS

All published by Alfred A. Knopf, Inc.
501 Madison Avenue, New York

THOMAS MANN

BY HENRY HATFIELD

REVISED EDITION

A NEW DIRECTIONS PAPERBOOK

To Victor A. Oswald, Jr.

Originally published in the *Makers of Modern
Literature Series* in 1951. First published as New
Directions Paperbook 101 in 1961. Revised paperback
edition, 1962.

Manufactured in the United States of America.
New Directions Books are published for James Laughlin
by New Directions Publishing Corporation,
333 Sixth Avenue, New York 10014

Third Printing

CONTENTS

CONTENTS

FOREWORD TO THE REVISED EDITION

FOREWORD TO THE REVISED EDITION

THE YEARS SINCE THOMAS MANN'S DEATH IN 1955 HAVE
brought neither a striking decline nor, as far as I can see,
a dramatic rise in his American reputation. A few interesting books have appeared: Erich Heller's *The Ironic
German,* Fritz Kaufmann's study of Mann's philosophical
ideas, and the competent if brief general British works
by Lindsay and Thomas. It seems however that Mann
no longer occupies a central position in critical discussion
and is in danger of becoming an academic subject in
this country, treated mainly in innocuous little articles in
learned journals. This would be disquieting; but if it is
mainly students who read Mann, one can reflect that
they are not the least sensitive group of readers in our
public. Not everything written around the universities is
necessarily "academic." It is also interesting that so
special a work as the *Story of a Novel,* Mann's own account of the origin and the intentions of his *Doctor
Faustus,* has been widely reviewed.

FOREWORD TO THE REVISED EDITION

In Germany, as far as I can judge, Mann's standing is now very high. *Felix Krull* and the *Essay on Schiller* were both tremendous successes. To put it nastily, one can say that the Germans have at last forgiven Mann for having been right about Hitler. Death is a great reconciler.

It is pleasant to record that a great many students in German universities read Mann, often with sensitivity and understanding. The generation born during the Nazi period is keenly interested in those elements of the German tradition which its parents rejected and almost destroyed. Mann has survived the ordeal of becoming a classic writer whose stories are analyzed and "interpreted" almost to death. Despite the fact that he is now an "official" author—shades of Gustave von Aschenbach! —Mann still interests and excites young people. Perhaps he seems a bit old-fashioned to them, compared to Kafka, Musil, and Broch; but he is still very much alive. Even in that dark wasteland, the "German Democratic Republic," his works are read and discussed.

To the first edition of this book I have added an eighth chapter, dealing with the more important works published between 1951 and 1955. The biographical sketch has been slightly changed; the bibliography considerably. A few mistakes have been corrected. With a certain ironic enjoyment, Thomas Mann himself pointed out my two worst slips: Goethe is not actually present in the final scene of *The Beloved Returns*; Lotte speaks to an hallucination. The essay *Freud and the Future*, which I found tactlessly concerned with Mann's own work, was received enthusiastically by Freud himself. Mann's "tendency towards the encyclopedic," mildly deprecated by me, has since been rightly interpreted as a useful element of his work. As Miss E. M. Wilkinson has shown, Mann, by providing in his works the aesthetic semblance of specialized knowledge, expressed an integral part of modern life.

Perhaps the most serious defect of my first edition was an occasional error in tone. At times the book is (or was) simply not positive enough. While not insensitive to the power of *Doctor Faustus*, I devoted too much attention to its defects, real or alleged; similarly, my discussion of *The Beloved Returns* was too cool and reserved. (There is no reason to retract any of the praise devoted to *Buddenbrooks, The Magic Mountain, Joseph,* or the great novellas.)

Writing a decade ago, I consciously avoided that tone of uncritical, humorless enthusiasm which still prevailed in some places. The American Mann cult which flourished in the Thirties and Forties did Mann's reputation more harm than good. My error was a natural one, but, as a colleague once observed, leaning over backwards is not the most graceful of positions. The stance of this edition is closer to the vertical. The proper study of mankind is Mann!

In addition to those persons mentioned in the Preface, I should like to thank Robert MacGregor and Herbert Steiner; Charles Neider for stimulating agreements and disagreements; and above all, Hermann Weigand, the dean of all students of Mann, for frank but generous criticism.

H. H.

August, 1961

PREFACE

Anyone who becomes sufficiently interested in Thomas Mann to turn to the critics and literary historians for enlightenment is likely to be struck by two things: the great bulk of material on hand and the paucity of intelligent criticism devoted to Mann's works as literature. There are various reasons for this state of affairs. A number of commentators stress the ideological "problems" in Mann's books so heavily that their critiques sound like algebra texts. Many of the German discussions are vitiated by political prejudice. On the other hand, Mann has suffered, though probably less than Rilke or Kafka, from pontifical and humorless admirers who have tried to make his work the center of a cult. Far from helping his reputation, this rather stuffy hero-worship has recently led, at least in America, to a sharp and often excessive reaction against it. Some useful comments have been made from the point of view of psychoanalysis and myth, but these methods are rarely used with finesse or restraint. Both rely heavily on association, and it is notorious that a reasonably clever person can prove anything by association.

This book aims to provide a critical account of Thomas Mann's novels and stories. I have tried to treat the various works as aesthetic units, each with its own "central intention," against the background of Mann's general development. After some hesitation, I decided against including any explicit discussion of Mann's essays—except of the *Reflections of a Non-Political Man,* which has never been translated—in the body of the book. A brief note at the end gives an account of some of the more important essays. It seems to me that Mann's critical papers, fascinating though some of them are, are far less relevant to his position as a "maker of modern literature" than is his fiction. Many of them are most valuable as comments on his novels and novellas, and I have used them from that point of view.

For encouragement and advice, I am grateful to Harry Levin, who first suggested that I write this study, and to Barker Fairley, André von Gronicka, James Laughlin, Golo Mann, Joan Merrick, Victor A. Oswald, Jr., Alfred Puhan, Hallett Smith, and Jack M. Stein. Without the hospitality of Margaret and Eli Sobel and Nina and Victor Oswald, writing the book would have been a far less pleasant experience. Thomas Mann graciously answered various questions about his work and gave me permission to use a recent photograph as the frontispiece of this book. Miss Ann Nedderman gave me valuable help in preparing the manuscript for publication. Finally, I must thank my wife for assistance of the most varied kind.

PREFACE

So much has been written about Mann that it is hard to avoid unconscious plagiarism; but my conscious borrowings from earlier critics are recorded in the Notes. I should like particularly to acknowledge my obligation to Hermann J. Weigand's study of *The Magic Mountain* and Käte Hamburger's commentary on *Joseph and His Brothers;* also to Vernon Venable's essay about *Death in Venice*, to the late Ernst Cassirer's article on *Lotte in Weimar*, and to Fred S. Heumann's unpublished study of the Hebrew sources of *Joseph*.

I am also obliged to the editors of the *University of Toronto Quarterly* for allowing me to use my essay on *Buddenbrooks*, in slightly revised form, in this book; to the Viking Press for permission to quote from Alma Mahler's *Gustav Mahler;* and to Alfred A. Knopf, Inc., for granting me the right to use a quotation from Willa Cather's *Not Over Forty* and some passages of Mann's works in Mrs. H. T. Lowe-Porter's and Denver Lindley's translations. My specific debts to Mrs. Lowe-Porter are listed in the Notes; the other translations from Mann are my own.

H. H.

New York, 1951

1. INTRODUCTION

The Quiet Revolutionary

AMONG THE MAJOR WRITERS OF THIS CENTURY, THOMAS Mann appears at first glance as perhaps the most conservative. One finds few if any startling affirmations; rather, a slow, painful groping towards a synthesis, or more often a weighing of antithetical extremes. Nor is the reader likely to find Mann's work obviously experimental. Mann's world is often complicated but seldom private: his use of symbols is at least relatively simple; one need only think of Joyce, Kafka, or Eliot, and the contrast is clear enough. There would seem to be no need for a key to the *Joseph* stories, for instance, let alone to *Tonio Kröger*. A critique is indeed badly needed; a guidebook, if at all, only for his very latest work.

If then there are new directions in Mann, they are not obviously indicated. They exist nevertheless; the cautious bourgeois is an explorer, as bourgeois often are. For all his deceptive air of conservatism, there is in Mann an almost Faustian urge to experiment, to go beyond. The author of *Buddenbrooks* might well have devoted himself, a German Zola, to a long series of family novels. Or, after *Tristan*, Mann might have confined himself exclusively to ingenious variations on the theme of the artist; for a long while, there seemed to be considerable danger of just that. Yet in *The Magic Mountain* the theme of the artist is subordinate; we have the novel of ideas on the grand scale. Then, after years of preparation, appears a new body of work by a writer in his sixties: *Joseph* and *The Beloved Returns*, novels of myth and psychology, which have more in common than is evident at first reading. And while *Doctor Faustus* takes up long-familiar themes, its total effect is radically different from that of any of Mann's earlier works.

Regarded as a whole, Mann's career is a striking example of the "repeated puberty" which Goethe thought characteristic of the genius. In technique as well as in thought, he experimented far more daringly than is generally realized. In *Buddenbrooks* he wrote one of the last of the great "old-fashioned" novels, a patient, thorough tracing of the fortunes of a family. The novel, far from naturalistic in spirit, demonstrates his mastery of the techniques of naturalism and impressionism: elaborate accounts of the dinners, the bank balances, and the ailments of the Buddenbrooks alternate with swift evocations of mood. Primarily—and hence no doubt its enormous popularity—the novel tells a story, in a solid, conventional, unilinear way. From *The Magic Mountain* on, the secure ground of the nineteenth-century novel has been left for good. Daring experiments with the time sense, lack of interest, for long periods, in narration as such, and mythical associations are characteristic. In the climactic chapter of *The Beloved Returns* Mann uses the technique of the stream of consciousness, which he ventures to apply to the mind of Goethe. Still more audacious is the attempt, in *Doctor Faustus*, to render in words the spirit and the impact of both actual and imaginary works of music. All of the later novels are in some sense experimental. Mann says somewhere that the great novel transcends the limits of the genre; this, like so many of his general statements, probably refers primarily to his own work.

Impressive as is the scope achieved by this transcendence, it is gained at times by a considerable aesthetic sacrifice, most strikingly in his strong tendency towards the encyclopedic. Mann ranged from anatomy to the occult, from entomology to counterpoint. If he did not take all knowledge for his province, he often suggests the ambitions of an intellectual imperialist.

In Mann's development of the symphonic novel, with a structure based on anticipation, repetition, and variation, there is the same tendency towards increased range of experimentation. The leitmotif, as Mann first used it, was nothing new in German literature. The repetition of a few words to characterize a given person or situation was a technique well understood by Otto Ludwig and Fontane; Mann might have hit upon it even without knowing Wagner. Gradually, almost imperceptibly, the leitmotif is used both more subtly and more extensively until in *Joseph* or *Doctor Faustus* a whole situation may be repeated, more or less varied; or a basic type of character returns under another name: Ishmael as Esau, Abraham as Jacob. Here as elsewhere Mann appears as a quiet revolutionary in literature; all the more effective, perhaps, for his outer conformity.

To emphasize only the new in Mann, however, would be grossly misleading. Few writers have been as conscious of tradition; few have stressed so insistently their relation to tradition. In Mann's case, the dominant early influences came from extra-literary sources: Schopenhauer, Wagner, Nietzsche, and later Freud. As Mann gradually shifted away from nineteenth-century romanticism and pessimism, he turned increasingly to an older strain in German culture, without completely repudiating his former guides. The figure of Goethe, both as man and artist, became increasingly significant to him. In varying ways, the major novels which follow *The Magic Mountain* reflect this significance. One senses in them, as in various essays, the *imitatio Goethe* carried to the point of emulation, even at times to identification.

Mann's work stands out from the mass of contemporary German literature above all because of its combination of great intellectual range and distinction and finesse of style. Other German novelists have made experiments on a monumental scale—one thinks of Döblin or Hermann Broch, for instance; still others, like Kafka, are perhaps his peers as stylists; it is Mann's fusion of matter and manner which is unique. Beyond this, and more precisely, his flair for psychology, his use of a pattern of subtle relationships within the frame of each work, and his solid, careful craftsmanship further distinguish his writings. His psychological vision, sharpened by Nietzsche, the Russian and the French novel, and later by Freud, is of a keenness which the German novel has rarely equaled. One thinks particularly of his characterizations of children. Hanno Buddenbrook at school, Ellie in *Disorder and Early Sorrow,* young Joseph beneath the moon—these are figures not unworthy of Proust.

It may be objected that Mann's "pattern"—the use of anticipation, repetition, and variation which goes far beyond the leitmotif—is complicated rather than subtle. There is some truth in the charge: thus some of the motifs in *Buddenbrooks* are repeated to the point of weariness. Here too there is a development. The use of the pencil-symbol to connect Hippe and Clavdia in *The Magic Mountain* is clear without being over-obvious; it requires a keener reader to sense, for example, the relation between the two enigmatic guides, jackal-god and angel, in the *Joseph* stories, to say nothing of some of the incredible finesses of *Doctor Faustus.* At his best, Mann is indeed "the old magician"; we sense perhaps that clever tricks have been used, but are diverted from looking into matters too closely.

Besides the internal patterns, there are numerous threads which link the various narratives and give a broad unity to his work as a whole. Most obvious are the connections among the host of artist figures. Or the protagonist of a sketch of 1904 (*At the Prophet's*) reappears as a minor yet significant figure in *Doctor Faustus.* The figure of Goethe "returns" more than once, with his almost fabulous charm and his precarious synthesis of spirit and life. Other lines run from the works of fiction to the essays: thus Peeperkorn, vital, charismatic, and not too bright, bears a certain resemblance to Mann's concept of Tolstoi.

5

One of the most basic of Mann's characteristics is the conscientious thoroughness often attributed to the Germans in general. "Only the thorough is truly interesting," he writes in the programmatic introduction to *The Magic Mountain.* The same attitude underlies the patient documentation of *Buddenbrooks* and the careful research which preceded *Joseph* and *Lotte in Weimar;* the psyche and the myth are scrutinized as carefully as is the skin of Clavdia Chauchat or the eccentric nature of the dog Bashan. In the world of ideas, Naphta and Settembrini would seem to neglect no possible stroke in their endless antithetical fencing. The solidity, the undeniable distinction of Mann's work come in no small degree from this thoroughness. Yet the defects of this virtue are no less real for being obvious: sheer Wagnerian bulk, and a tendency to digressions which are not always fascinating in their own right. The chapter "Operationes Spirituales" in *The Magic Mountain* shows by example as well as by precept that endless intellectual gymnastics lead inevitably to mental fatigue.

Mann's self-consciousness, extraordinary even in our time, would seem to spring from the same psychological ground as his anxious attention to detail. All his works, to some degree, are "portraits of the artist," and even much of his criticism falls into the same category. (Here one has a right to complain: it is one thing to find Thomas Mann behind the mask of Aschenbach or even of Moses; another to be presented with a Goethe cast largely in his image.) Mann had more right than most to quote Ibsen's dictum that writing means sitting in judgment on oneself. His castigation of the artist as parasite, criminal, and demagogue would have satisfied Plato at his most puritanical. Even Joseph, who is something of an artist, is also something of a rogue. Like his model Goethe, Mann characteristically exaggerates his sense of guilt in order to attain a sense of psychic relief. Werther and Aschenbach die in order that their creators may live. In both, there is the pattern of confession and catharsis. Mann's *Reflections of a Non-Political Man* is an example of the same process; conservative political romanticism and nationalism are carried to hectic extremes—and are eventually overcome. In the same way, Mann purged himself of the early conviction of his own decadence and to some extent even of his obsession with the "problem of the artist." No one who comes to know himself, Mann tells us, remains the same person that he was. (Mann's belief that the artist is somehow inferior to the "normal" person, and unable to cope with the good, practical *Bürger*, seems a bit naive and should not be mistaken for a universal truth. Chaucer, Milton, and Shakspere, to go no further, are exceptions worth noting.)

Whether literally artists or not, all Mann's heroes are of course "marked men," and marked, with very few exceptions, in a sinister sense. Generally they are threatened by illness of some sort; and Mann's deepest sympathy is with the "heroes of creative work," the *Leistungsethiker* who like Thomas Buddenbrook, Aschenbach, and Schiller work at "the edge of exhaustion" and often succumb to tasks beyond their strength. Nowhere is Mann more indebted to the German romantics, especially to Novalis, than in his conception of genius as disease, of art and spirit as the enemies of life. Such views were also in line with the spirit of the 1880's and '90's: Lombroso's association of genius with insanity, Max Nordau's facile jeremiads about degeneracy, and the general belief of the European *fin de siècle* that decadence was the order of the day.

The Divided Mind

The dualism implicit in Mann's view of the artist is basic in all of his thought. Convinced that monism is a "boring" philosophy, he divides the universe into a glittering series of polar opposites, of which the opposition of spirit to life is the most fundamental; the antithesis artist-*Bürger* is only a corollary. When one realizes that for "spirit" one can substitute art, death, illness, or love; for "life" nature, the normal, the material, or the naive, a certain looseness in Mann's mode of thought becomes obvious enough. This thinking in antitheses lends a dramatic flair: often two contrasted characters (or ideas) illuminate each other reciprocally. One thinks of Tonio Kröger and Hans Hansen, Naphta and Settembrini, Goethe and Schiller. Yet arbitrarily to declare certain ideas "polar opposites"—as in Mann's notorious contrast between *Kultur* and civilization—and then to play one against the other like a virtuoso, can lead to confusion and intellectual irresponsibility. In the *Reflections of a Non-Political Man*, for example, a *tour de force* of this type of thinking, the author often appears as a word-intoxicated man.

In the history of ideas, the predecessors of Mann's antithetical mode of thought were Nietzsche, the German romanticists, and Schiller, whose essay "On Naive and Reflective Poetry" Mann profoundly admired. Other, more personal influences may however have been more decisive. In *Tonio Kröger* and elsewhere, Mann speaks of a racial mixture—his North German father and a mother with Creole blood—as a force which produced a sharp split in his view of life, impelling him towards a certain dualism from the womb, as it were. More satisfying than this dubious biological theory is the explanation afforded by his intellectual and social position. The dichotomy in his own nature between the artist and the descendant of a patrician Lübeck family has been treated by Mann in numerous variations and discussed *ad nauseam* by his interpreters. At least equally significant, though relatively neglected, is the tension between the German romantic tradition and the European, cosmopolitan strain which runs throughout his work. On the one hand, Mann, by his own repeated statements, is the follower of a romantic, pessimistic, and deeply conservative tendency in German thought; musical rather than logical; and significantly enough, an admirer of such an enormously sentimental story as Storm's *Immensee*. Yet as the author of *Buddenbrooks* he is the pupil of European naturalism, as such of a predominantly logical, rationalistic, and "scientific" movement. Politically he is equally torn; his *Frederick and the Great Coalition* and other war books defend the Prussianism he had elsewhere treated ironically. The duel in *The Magic Mountain* symbolizes, among other things, the clash between the two sides of Mann's heritage. It will not do, of course, to construct an absolute antithesis between the German and the Western European. The greatest Germans are Europeans too; it is no accident that Joseph, Mann's most ambitious attempt at a synthesis of

9

spirit and life, bears a certain resemblance to young Goethe. But the tension between the two elements remains. The *Joseph* stories mark the extreme of his flight from a Germany grown distasteful, while in *Doctor Faustus* there is a symbolic exile's return to the German scene, but a return marked by anguish.

For many reasons, then, Mann's view of the world is profoundly dualistic. Attracted to the "spirit" and to life, to art and the middle class, he seems to have found it equally difficult to cast in his lot finally with either side. In this dualism lies the source of Mann's irony: life is attracted to spirit, spirit to life; the artist longs, with "the least bit of scorn" for "the bliss of the ordinary." Mann's divided view of the world, which characteristically results in ambiguities and ambivalences, has irritated some readers. But his irony, like Voltaire's, is "no cruel goddess." An ironic attitude towards human characters does not exclude real warmth towards them; one thinks of Toni Buddenbrook, Hans Castorp, and Serenus Zeitblom in *Doctor Faustus*.

Yet in the ironic treatment of ideas Mann is sometimes less happy. One grows impatient with his refusal to commit himself; what, for example, is one's attitude towards the values represented by Peeperkorn in *The Magic Mountain* supposed to be? Here too there has been a development. While ironies still abound, they become less decisive, intellectually. More and more, in his fiction as well as in his essays, Mann takes a humanistic and "Western" position. *Doctor Faustus,* in many ways a return to the German "side," shares its forthrightness with the later political essays. Despite its many ironies, it is unique

10

among Mann's novels in the degree of its commitment to a fixed system of standards.

Throughout his literary career, or series of careers, covering over fifty years, Mann's evolution has been gradual but complicated. Perhaps there is no better way to follow the dialectic of traditionalist and innovator, German and European, artist and bourgeois, in Mann's development than to examine his writings, more or less chronologically, from his first, rather slight short stories to his latest novel. And since Mann has consistently subordinated his "outer" life to his work, while his work, on the other hand, is always in some sense autobiographical, this examination should result in something like his inner biography.

2. COMEDY AND WRETCHEDNESS

MANN HAD SEVERAL CAREERS AS A CREATIVE ARTIST. THE
first, ended by the First World War, is made most memorable by *Buddenbrooks* and a brilliant succession of short
stories; the second, the period of the Weimar Republic,
is dominated by *The Magic Mountain;* finally, the time of
his exile is marked by mythical and parodistic works like
Joseph, Doctor Faustus, and *Felix Krull.* It is hard to make
any neat arrangement of the short stories and novellas,
culminating in *Death in Venice,* of his "first" career. As
everyone knows, nearly all of them deal with the "marked
man," literally or symbolically the artist, in his relation
to life. Yet a fairly definite change in mood and in tem-
per divides most of the earlier stories from *Tonio Kröger*
(1903) and many of the narratives which follow it. Disregarding for the moment the three youthful stories which
Mann has excluded from the collections, one finds that
most of the earlier stories are coolly and sharply drawn,
deeply and often bitterly pessimistic. From *Tonio* on,

the tone of the most significant works shifts; the artist finds pleasure in what he sees in the mirror, and there is often a lyric note in the self-descriptions. Both the artist and "life" have gained a new status: thus *Royal Highness, A Weary Hour, Death in Venice,* and even, paradoxically, *Felix Krull.* A purely chronological division is impossible, as the earlier strain persists after the narcissistic note has been sounded, but broadly speaking the early stories deal, rather mordantly, with the "comedy and wretchedness" which the young Tonio Kröger saw everywhere.

By contrast, the youthful pieces which Mann later rejected, like *Fallen* (1894), *The Will to Happiness* (1896), and *Death* (1897), seem relatively undisciplined in their treatment of emotion. Yet while these stories are all more or less sentimental, betraying the immature pupil of Heine and Theodor Storm, their style is unexpectedly clean and precise. *Fallen,* which appeared in the naturalistic magazine *Die Gesellschaft,* brought Mann a warmly encouraging letter from the poet Richard Dehmel. Written in an impressionistic manner, with short, nervous sentences, the story treats the "problem of the fallen woman," so dear to the time, in an ironic and remarkably conservative way. To refute the "modern" views of a freethinking student, an older man tells the story of an actress who gives herself first to her young lover, then to an unprepossessing older man. "If a woman falls for the sake of love today, she will fall for the sake of money tomorrow." Despite this adolescent cynicism, the account of the lover's disillusionment has a sharp, "felt" quality. *The Will to Happiness* culminates in the *Liebestod* of the painter

13

Paolo Hofmann. His half-southern, half-German name marks him as a close relative of Tonio Kröger, but it is less as the artist that he interests Mann than as a bizarre martyr of love, the first of his "heroes of accomplishment." A hopeless invalid, Hofmann has been forbidden to marry. Yet he waits five years for his sweetheart, staying alive only by a grim exertion of the will, and dies on the morning after his wedding. This is the most obvious of Mann's plots, and it is not surprising that he has repudiated the story, but it has passages with an exactness of observation reminiscent of Dürer:

> [After an illness] his temples and cheeks showed even more distinctly than usual the pale blue network of veins which one can often observe in delicate brunette people.

Death, a brief story in diary form, is remarkable mainly for Mann's ironic counterpointing of reality against the ideal; for death, romantically imagined as beautiful and majestic, appears as "dry, boring, and bourgeois."

To turn to the stories which have become part of the canon: they are, almost without exception, variations on a single theme, but it is precisely the variation, the individuality of each novella, that is of first importance. The basic contrast between the isolated individual and the normal majority is easy enough to grasp; and if one focuses on it, the tendency is to reduce all the narratives to a rather wearying monotony, to accuse Mann of repetitiousness or even of sterility. Clearly, the fault lies more in the interpreters than in the author. Even a completely naive approach, which would regard Herr Friedemann or Praisegod Piepsam, for instance, simply as "real people," as

14

human beings with definitely marked physical and psychological traits, would be more fruitful than the abstract interpretation which emphasizes again and again that Friedemann or Piepsam represents "the spirit" or the artist. This more or less official reading is of course correct on its own level and does have considerable relevance, but when it is made central, it leads one away from the works themselves. At its worst, it degenerates into pseudo-philosophy. Whatever Mann's importance as a thinker—and many of his critics seem to discuss the "philosophy" of his stories with a certain pontifical overseriousness—the works can best be read as literature; the artistic *how* is at least as interesting as the ideological *what*. With Mann one cannot afford to neglect either.

Particularly in the stories which precede *Tonio Kröger*, Mann is engaged in a sort of two-front war: "life" and its healthy representatives are dull or brutal or both; but the antagonists to "life," the isolated and introspective protagonists, are sick, psychologically maladjusted, and frequently grotesque. The negativism of Mann's position is obvious enough: what one respects is the honesty and consistency with which he maintains it. With this view of the world, a certain cruelty is inevitable, and the "lovelessness" with which the heroine of *Royal Highness* later reproaches the prince (a symbol of the author) comes out clearly in many of the works themselves. There is a certain patrician scorn implied in the hardness and ugliness of Mann's portrayals, yet he describes his own type more harshly than any other. The treatment of emotion is incisive and analytic rather than sensuous; a sense of "distance" and objectivity is preserved. One sees Tobias Mindernickel kill his dog, one believes in the affair between Amra Jacoby and the musician Läutner, and is keenly interested; but the narrator does not seem particularly moved by these events. Neither is the reader, consciously at least, but he is not likely to forget them.

The most remarkable thing about the early works is their keenness of psychological insight. Writing in his twenties, the author neither has nor claims to have any vast range of experience; but what he has seen, he has seen clearly. Mann's dissections of the artist, or near-artist, have long been famous, but what is even more impressive is his penetration into characters to which he has little, if any, autobiographical relation. One thinks of the "trembling cruelty" of the curiously compounded Gerda (in *Little Herr Friedemann*), or of how Jacoby, in *Little Lizzie*, stammers guiltily "Please excuse me!" after a painful accident in which he has been the innocent and injured person. The young fanatic in *Gladius Dei*, or the dilettante in the story of that name, with his knowledge of anxiety and its causes, and of "that hatred which is nothing but a poisoned love," inevitably come to mind. One may infer that Mann had a debt to the Russians for his ability to penetrate into the lower strata of the mind, to the French for the dry, usually unsentimental character of his psychology, to Nietzsche for its skeptical orientation, particularly as concerns the artist; yet his psychological talent remains an amazing and fundamentally inexplicable endowment.

The style of these stories is an admirably appropriate one. Generally, a few details are shown accurately but rapidly. The sentences, on the whole simpler and shorter than in Mann's later works, are precise and give the effect of hitting the mark. Parallel to this sparseness of style is an economy of means especially unusual in German literature; thus Mann expresses the futility of Herr Friedemann's business career merely by mentioning his "office" in quotation marks.

From the first, Mann employs the leitmotif effectively. Compared to the subtlety with which the device is handled in later works, its use in the stories which precede *Buddenbrooks* often seems mechanical and obvious. Yet the repetition of "gray" in *Little Herr Friedemann*, for instance, combined as it is with words like "faded," "gentle," and "faint" which have a "gray" emotional tone, establishes the tone economically and with finality.

Disillusionment, a sketch of 1896, contains the quintessence of the early Mann. A gentleman of uncertain age, encountered in Venice, tells in a few pages of his experiences. Compared to the "big words" of the poets, all of them have been pitifully anticlimactic; life is a miserable disappointment after the great expectations which literature has irresponsibly aroused "Is that all there is?" or "What does that amount to anyway?" is his reaction to disaster, to his first view of the sea, to love. Still more characteristic than this leitmotif is the note of isolation and of a certain self-pity; the reference to *Werther* is significant. "I have become lonely, unhappy, and a bit strange . . . ," the gentleman remarks; obviously, he too is a psychological ancestor of Tonio Kröger.

Little Herr Friedemann (1897) is sharper, cooler, and more mature. From the beginning, *in medias res*—"It was the nurse's fault," to the final scene, the story shows a striking gain in technical competence. Friedemann, crippled in infancy, has renounced "life" and achieved a sort of precarious equilibrium as an amateur of the arts, especially of music, and, within his narrow limits, an epicure. Gerda von Rinnlingen, herself a lover of music, marked as a decadent, in Mann's rather stereotyped fashion, by bluish shadows below her eyes, destroys Friedemann by fostering and then scorning his grotesque love for her. His suicide is made inevitable by her deliberate humiliation of him; yet Gerda, in whom sensuality and fastidiousness, sensitivity and sadism, are credibly combined, is not made the object of any moral judgment; a sort of naturalistically conceived decadence is responsible for her actions as well as for his. One notes as characteristic the autobiographical background (the "commercial city of medium size" is obviously Lübeck); the use of Wagner's music, and of the notion that music is a sinister force; the flirtation with numerology (Friedemann's fateful encounter with Gerda is in Box 13 at the opera, a painfully obvious touch); and the use of water as a symbol of release and death.

1897 was something of an *annus mirabilis* for Mann; it saw the completion of *The Dilettante, Tobias Mindernickel,* and *Little Lizzie* as well as of *Friedemann.* The "dilettante," who has fallen between the stools of business and art, is a sort of antitype of the artist, or of Mann himself. He has the same divided heritage, but in him the result is merely a half-talent for improvisation; he is completely sterile. The same type reappears in Christian Buddenbrook, and may well represent an obsessive fear of Mann's: "There, but for the grace of God . . ." In family background, in his rejection of the Bohemian, above all in his feeling of painful inferiority to the bourgeois-normal, the dilettante is a caricature, if not a portrait of the artist. Rather significantly, it is one of the very few stories told in the first person.

Tobias Mindernickel and *Little Lizzie* are less obviously symbolic than is usual in Mann's work; they exist more in their own right, and perhaps for that reason have more sharpness than most of the other stories. Mindernickel (the first half of whose very grotesque name suggests inferiority), a person of fabulously ridiculous looks, cannot appear on the street without encountering shouts of mockery. A compound of masochist and sadist, he can love only those even more miserable than he. His killing of his cherished dog is one of the most convincingly unpleasant moments in German literature. In *Little Lizzie,* the lawyer Jacoby is equally pathological. Like many of Mann's early "heroes" he despises himself, but to a unique degree. Mann portrays Jacoby in his spiritual inferiority and elephantine corpulence with an unflinching realism bordering on cruelty, but cannot refuse a certain sympathy to one who is sick in body and mind. (One of his most persistent prejudices, inherited from German romanticism, was that illness is more interesting and "deeper" than health.) Jacoby is afflicted with a chronic bad conscience, arising apparently from a conviction of his insufficiency as a husband. His wife Amra, a sensual, beautiful, and completely ruthless woman with "voluptuously indolent gestures," is of course not bothered by considerations of conscience. Healthy and amoral, she may be said to represent "life," while her sick, self-conscious, anxiety-ridden husband sym-

19

bolizes the spirit. Amra has for her devoted husband the hatred of the healthy Nietzschean animal for the diseased; the humiliation which she devises for him leads directly to his death. Since woman is considered to be closer than man to nature and "life," she is more dangerous, as Gerda, in *Little Herr Friedemann,* also reminds us.

Mann had read Nietzsche about 1895, and the succession of blond, healthy, and often brutal "life" figures in his stories represents one of his more obvious debts to that philosopher. The obsessive belief that music is a sinister force, running from *Little Herr Friedemann* through *Doctor Faustus,* is another. *"Cave musicam!"* Nietzsche had proclaimed, and it is no accident that music furnishes the means by which Amra and her lover dispose of Jacoby. The analysis of musical effects in the same critical scene shows considerable technical knowledge, on which Mann drew repeatedly in later works.

The Wardrobe (1899), a sort of fairy tale of great and tantalizing charm, is unique in Mann's work and particularly unexpected in his realistic period. "Everything must remain uncertain" is its leitmotif, and this truly neoromantic precept is consistently observed. Albrecht van der Qualen, who has only a few more months to live, has resolutely cut himself off from contact with external reality. When, on a sudden impulse, he leaves the Berlin-Rome express, he knows only that he is in some German city, and that it is "more or less" autumn. Yet this dreamlike freedom from space and time leads to no vagueness of presentation; the total effect is largely achieved by scenes of precise observation. *The Wardrobe* is also one of Mann's most effectively understated stories. Van der

Qualen, crossing a bridge, observes a "long, decaying skiff . . . in the stern was a man propelling it with a long pole." Van der Qualen is indeed close to death, for the boatman is Charon, though the casual reader is not likely to realize his identity.

In its mixture of the photographic and the fantastic, *The Wardrobe* has some affinity to Kafka, and it is not surprising that the protagonist thinks of E. T. A. Hoffmann. Essentially, however, the story is closer to Hans Christian Andersen, for it is lyrical as well as uncanny. In the room which van der Qualen finds stands a very prosaic wardrobe. Whether the lovely girl who appears in it and tells him stories in the vein of a folk-song or fairy tale "stands for" art, or life, or the Muse, is a question which does not affect the fascination of the brief novella. It reveals a talent in Mann for dealing with the non-rational and "otherworldly" which is too often ignored. Slight though it is, it contains Mann's first evocation of the world of classical myth. When he returned to that world, in *Death in Venice* or in the chapter "Snow" in *The Magic Mountain,* his work was at its greatest.

The name van der Qualen immediately suggests torture or torment to the German reader. This device of significant naming is frequently employed by Mann. Besides Mindernickel, one thinks of Piepsam, a word evocative of the futile chirpings of a bird; of the obstetrician Mecum and of Schimmelpreester (priest of mould) in *Felix Krull;* of Frau Stöhr, whose name expresses her annoying character, and Herr Wehsal (Mr. Misery!) in *The Magic Mountain,* and so on.

The Way to the Churchyard (1901) marks a return

from the fantastic sphere of *The Wardrobe* to Mann's usual realm. The unhappy Praisegod Piepsam, a completely isolated and frustrated person, is disturbed by a cyclist on his way to visit the graves of his family, falls into an impotent fury, and collapses. As we are all too clearly informed, the cyclist is "life," going along the predestined, normal path. "Life's" leitmotif is "flashing blue eyes"—a symbol for the healthy burgher which Mann employs to and beyond the point of triteness.

Gladius Dei (1902) is the first story which clearly reflects the milieu of Munich, where Mann made his home from 1893 until his voluntary exile in 1933. In the first decades of this century, Munich was perhaps the greatest center of German letters, and certainly of German art, and Mann has caught the aura of brilliance and aesthetic excitement which the Bavarian capital then possessed. In a sense, *Gladius Dei* is another story of the artist and of the play of antithetical forces, but it has a vivid individuality of its own. The Bohemian Munich of the turn of the century is described with affection and irony. The Lübeck patrician is of course too sophisticated to be shocked by its easy *mores,* but he finds them problematic and a bit sloppy. "We are no gypsies in a green wagon," as Tonio Kröger was to put it. Rapidly and with humor, Mann shows how the worship of beauty and the cult of art dominate the city. He cannot resist the enthusiasm—Munich in his description becomes a second Florence—but about the hegemony of the aesthetic, he is characteristically of two minds. A painter has used his mistress as the model for a very fleshly, technically brilliant Madonna; against the display of this work the monklike

Jerome, a lank, haggard figure, remonstrates. This reincarnated Savonarola is quickly ejected from the art-store where he has made his protest, but there is a hint at the end of his eventual triumph: "Gladius Dei super terras, cito et velociter." The story is one of Mann's finest: the creation of the Munich atmosphere, the realization of the minor figures as well as of "Savonarola," above all the handling of the antithesis of the aesthetic and the moral, the Bohemian and the ascetic, implicitly, without lengthy ideological disquisitions, are beyond praise. In the last regard, it is infinitely superior to the closet-drama *Fiorenza* (1904), which treats the same theme with Shavian wordiness unrelieved by Shavian wit.

Not that this long prose dialogue lacks intellectual interest or distinction. But Mann makes everything mercilessly explicit: the characters tend to speak for pages at a stretch, and even the jokes are carefully explained. The setting is late fifteenth-century Florence, with Lorenzo de'Medici cast as the great opponent of Savonarola. Again Mann is fascinated by the parallel, real or imagined, between the dying Renaissance and his own day; one occasionally has the impression of watching *fin-de-siècle* intellectuals in Italian costume. Lorenzo, the type of the aesthetic man, is defeated by the far less attractive Savonarola, and there is no doubt that the priest will wield the *gladius Dei*. Like some of Mann's other decadents, Lorenzo has been overcome by an inexplicable weariness. The age of art is reaching its end, beauty is no longer enough, and "morality is possible again." The future belongs to the ascetic and the fanatic.

At first glance, it would appear that Mann's arrange-

23

ment of ideological forces had radically shifted: here the artist is on the side of life. But Savonarola is essentially an artist too, and more gifted than his brilliant opponent. (He is also an apostle of social justice, and as such a forerunner of Naphta.) The clash is one of pagan art, love, and life against ascetic art, hatred, and death; there is intellect on both sides. Merely normal, unintelligent "life" (represented by the brother of Lorenzo) is considered to have no interest whatsoever; for once the "blond and blue-eyed" come off badly. Both Savonarola and his antagonist are physical weaklings who triumph despite their handicaps, as true Mannian heroes. Savonarola's asceticism is explained in Nietzschean terms as the result of a sexual rejection in youth; his actions, again like Naphta's, are motivated by hatred and resentment.

Mann is generally more successful in dealing with the contemporary than with the historical. When he transfers a theme from the mythical past to a modern setting and develops it with sophisticated finesse, he is often at his most brilliant. This was his procedure in *Tristan* (1902). Inevitably, the concept of the "love-death," with passion, music, and night arrayed against rationality and light, attracted him. Long before Wagner, Novalis in his *Hymns to Night* and Friedrich Schlegel in the heavily erotic novel *Lucinde* had associated the same cluster of symbols. Sexual relief from the tensions of existence is felt to be profoundly related to the release given by death, and only in death can lovers find lasting union and liberation from the world. While the core of Mann's *Tristan*, in line with the *Liebestod* tradition, is profoundly romantic, it is overlaid by strata in which a coolly objective, "scientific" atti-

24

tude prevails. There is an abundance of the sardonic and more than a touch of the grotesque: the world of the novella is tragicomic, or better tragi-ironic.

From another point of view, *Tristan* is a bridge between the sphere of North German burghers and that of *The Magic Mountain*. A middle-class family—the blond businessman Klöterjahn, his brunette, weary, and musical wife, and their blond and phenomenally healthy baby—are projected into a sanatorium. The wife, whose musical talent corresponds, in Mannian terms, to her tendency to tuberculosis, encounters in Detlev Spinell one of the less impressive incarnations of the artist; he is the author of one *précieux* book and presumably will never write another. Physically he is so repulsive that another of the patients describes him as "the decayed suckling." Yet in terms of the legend and of Mann's dialectic he must be and is Tristan, and he has after all the intellect and imaginative sympathy which the Hanseatic Babbitt cannot supply.

The opening pages treating the sanatorium, its staff, and its inmates are mordantly satiric. Spinell's qualifications for his role are slight indeed: even his virility is dubious. Surely, one feels, this is the least lyrical of Tristans; but one has reckoned without Wagner, and without Mann. Like E. T. A. Hoffmann's Antonia, Frau Klöterjahn, for reasons of health, has been forbidden to indulge in music. Spinell, to achieve a symbolic union with her, seduces her into playing for him. On the piano he finds the score of *Tristan und Isolde*. What follows is one of Mann's most spectacular *tours de force:* the evocation in a few pages of prose of the essence of the legend. Mann quotes and paraphrases liberally, but the total effect, gained by juxtaposing ironic realism and an ecstatic interpretation of Wagner's music, is a startlingly fresh one. The story has passed rapidly from satire to mystical eroticism:

> Here two forces, two beings, strove towards each other, in transports of joy and pain; here they embraced and became one in delirious yearning after eternity and the absolute.

As one might expect, the experience proves to be too much for Frau Klöterjahn: the "love-death" is fulfilled in a literal, though parodistic sense. Despite a stinging humiliation at the hands of the injured Klöterjahn, Spinell has had his triumph: his Isolde, in her last days, is estranged from her all too normal family. Yet "life," in the form of the jubilantly healthy baby, has the last word. *Tristan* is Mann's first parody, using the term, as he does, to mean the retelling of a myth from a modern, self-conscious point of view. In his latest works, from *The Tales of Jacob* through *Doctor Faustus*, he has returned to parody on a far more ambitious scale, but never with more virtuosity than in the early novella. If *Tristan* is not one of his great stories, it is a *locus classicus* for his early view of music and the artist, and of the world.

The Infant Prodigy (1903) is equally characteristic as far as it goes, but it is little more than a sketch, a brief variation on the usual theme. During the performance of a boy pianist, the reactions of various members of the audience are played off ironically against the thoughts of the "wonder child." The "distance" between performer and audience, professional and amateur, appears as a source of pathos as well as of irony, in a way which approaches the softer mood of *Tonio Kröger*.

A Gleam (1904) is another study of the relationship between the "two worlds," the citizens of "life" being, like Baron Harry, hard, ruthless, and in a crude way happy, while the children of the "spirit" are introverted and defenseless. The scene is a party at an officers' casino, where members of the nobility, the demi-monde, and a single member of the middle class are thrown together. Mann has a predilection for dances, concerts, and other festivities, for the isolation of the individual stands out most sharply at the occasions "where life holds its simple-minded fêtes." Here, each of a series of characters suffers from an unanswered love or infatuation for another, producing a rather obviously arranged, Heinesque situation. The brief, impressionistic story reaches a shocking, quite un-Mannian climax; then a sudden reversal gives the heroine her "gleam" of paradoxical happiness. In its treatment of the German officer class, *A Gleam* has something of the ironic realism which marks *At the Prophet's,* a sketch of the same year which is set in an intellectually pretentious and squalid stratum of Munich, made up of curious and rather repulsive Bohemians who mix philosophy and politics with their art in a very promiscuous way. The proclamations of a certain Daniel, one of the lesser satellites of Stefan George, are read with theatrical solemnity before an audience including a "philosopher who looked like a kangaroo," a female "expert on erotics," various other *avant-garde* types, and two relatively bourgeois outsiders, one of whom, the writer, is obviously Mann himself. Daniel's manifestoes, a brew of Nietzsche,

27

Stefan George, the New Testament, and expressions borrowed from military science, announce the coming of a conqueror called Christus Imperator Maximus. "Soldiers," the proclamation concludes, "I turn over to you for plundering—the world." Over forty years later, Mann included the episode in *Doctor Faustus*. Only a few details have been changed, but the tone is radically different: the prophet appears even more grotesque, but he is seen seriously, as a precursor of Nazism.

Mann has implied that *The Blood of the Walsungs* (1905) should be classed with his more "humorous" and "superficial" stories of the period, such as *The Railway Accident* and *The Fight between Jappe and Do Escobar*. But incest is not a particularly comic theme, and it seems better to take this uncompromising and brilliantly realized novella seriously, as one of the most consistently and skilfully worked-out products of European decadence. The story has a strange history: it was scheduled to appear in the *Neue Rundschau* in January, 1906, but the proofs were destroyed before publication. For many years it was not available in the original German, except in a privately printed edition, though it is accessible in French, as *Sang Reservé*, as well as in *Stories of Three Decades*. Perhaps Mann wished to keep the story, set in a German-Jewish milieu in Berlin, out of the hands of German anti-Semites.

Mann's Siegmund and Sieglinde are the brilliant and spoiled twin children of a self-made businessman. Witty and hypercritical, they have a private alliance against the rest of the world, not least against Sieglinde's commonplace fiancé von Beckerath. The twins always hold hands, "although their hands are moist." Sieglinde, whose "animal-like eyes" characterize her sufficiently, is not disturbed by the situation, but her brother has a compulsion to wash himself continually. He is the "marked man" of the story, an artist *manqué* who indulges in antitheses about creation and passion. A few days before Sieglinde's wedding, they make a sort of rite of witnessing the passion of their namesakes in *Die Walküre.* Like Spinell and Frau Klöterjahn in *Tristan,* they are moved by Wagner's music to enact a "parody" of the myth. After the event, Siegmund remarks that von Beckerath's existence "will be a little less trivial, from now on." With this line, the most devastatingly brutal in all of Mann, the novella closes. It gives a hint, perhaps, of a daemonic cynicism which he has rarely allowed himself to express. In the terms of *Doctor Faustus,* Zeitblom has nearly always kept Leverkühn in check. Mann has written here with an unsentimental hardness which one associates with French, rather than German decadence; he has achieved the kind of effect which his brother Heinrich often tried to produce.

The Fight between Jappe and Do Escobar (1911) is of course a far less ambitious piece, but in its way a highly successful one. It is an unpretentious account of a fight between two boys which shows Mann's very sensitive understanding of children and adolescents. The feelings of the narrator, a timid and imaginative "artist" type, who fears and yet hopes that he too will be drawn into combat, are especially well rendered.

Aside from *Tristan,* Mann's more realistic stories are not marked by any very striking technical innovations. The significant formal experiments are made rather in the full-length portraits of the artist like *Tonio Kröger* and *Death in Venice*. But after the turn of the century, a certain change in tone is perceptible in the narratives of either type. "Life," first regarded more or less as a ruthless Nietzschean beast, becomes partially domesticated and is often equated with middle-class normality. Despite *The Blood of the Walsungs,* the atmosphere becomes generally warmer, the irony less cutting. The isolation of the artist, never completely overcome, is mitigated: thus the writer in *At the Prophet's* is "on fairly good terms with life." Mann was beginning to accept the universe.

Along with purely biographical factors, the psychological catharsis afforded by writing *Buddenbrooks* may have had a good deal to do with Mann's gradual change in attitude, for his first novel had represented a very thorough coming to terms with his family heritage. Composed in an "age of nervous little sketches," it was also the first triumphant demonstration that Mann was a major writer.

3. THE WORLD OF THE FATHER

T. S. ELIOT ONCE REMARKED ON THE "USEFULNESS" OF A TYPE
of poetry "which could cut across all the present stratifica-
tions of public taste," and cited the plays of Shakspere,
with their "several layers of significance" as examples of
works of the desired universality of appeal. Eliot was writing only of poetry, but his *aperçu* illuminates the enormous success of *Buddenbrooks*. Essentially a rather complicated and deeply pessimistic book, it has an abundance
of sheer narration, of humor, of easily grasped character
and local color, which make its vast popularity natural
enough; and also a certain sympathetic warmth in dealing with character which is more agreeable to most readers than the cool temperature of the early novellas. One
need know nothing of Wagner or Schopenhauer, of the
theory of decadence or the metaphysical allure of death
to find the novel absorbing, and this is all to the good. Nor
need one have heard of the leitmotif to "get" the effect of
Mann's repetitions; indeed it would be difficult to miss

most of them. To say this is not, of course, to disparage the less obvious attractions of the book: its tendency and meaning, its overtones and associations. The comparison with Galsworthy's *Forsyte Saga*, sometimes facilely and misleadingly made, can be enlightening. *Buddenbrooks*, besides its "popular" elements, has precisely what the *Saga* does not: the broad range of "layers of significance," unexpected finesses, and a technique which, if at times obviously used, points ahead from the straightforward historical arrangement of nineteenth-century narration to the musical complexities of the novel of the twentieth century. Mann's own reference to Wagner's *Ring* furnishes a needed clue.

Despite his doubts about the bulk and nature of the book, Mann completed *Buddenbrooks* in about two and a half years; it was published early in 1901. The actual writing was begun in Italy, where he spent a year with his brother Heinrich. Yet there is no trace of the South in the novel. This was no "Italian journey" in Goethe's sense; it had nothing to do with the traditional attempt of the German writer to experience the Mediterranean and classic world; it was rather a period of deliberate self-isolation, which afforded no doubt perspective and concentration on his work. Mann tells us that his mood at the time was made up of "indolence, a bad conscience as a bourgeois, and the secure sense of latent talents." For the "bad conscience" there were presumably two reasons: his rejection of any sort of middle-class career, and his choice of the decay of his own family as a subject. At times, Mann must have felt that he was committing an indiscretion if not a downright betrayal. Thomas Buddenbrook is closely modeled after Mann's own father, and his exotic wife Gerda would seem, to a lesser extent, reminiscent of Mann's mother, Julia Da Silva-Bruhns. Psychologically, the novel may be said to represent a sort of reckoning with the father image by a young man who has broken with family tradition and gone off to carry on a "questionable" existence in Munich and Italy. He has rejected the ancestral firm, business, the whole world of Lübeck; his revolt has been successful and, outwardly, not very difficult, but a sense of guilt and remorse remains. The reckoning is unusually gentle, as such things go; the rejection reluctant. Sympathy and admiration for the father's world persist, and with them the chronic bad conscience of the Mannian hero. Without this ambivalence towards the burgher, so different from the harsh single-mindedness of Heinrich Mann, Mann's view of the world would be clearer and sharper, but his books cooler and less "felt." As he states in *Tonio Kröger,* the problematic love for the bourgeois world represented by his father (and arbitrarily called the "normal") was one of the strongest forces impelling him to write. The same emotion must have produced the psychological tension, the "charge," which saves *Buddenbrooks* from being only another family novel.

Buddenbrooks then is profoundly autobiographical, but it stands also in a European literary tradition. Mann had a great debt to his predecessors in the novel of the nineteenth century—Scandinavian, French, and Russian. From German writers, with one or two exceptions, he took little. Theodor Storm attracted him by a certain dexterity in the creation of a mood of sentimental reminiscence, and in

33

a not unskilful use of the leitmotif. Theodor Fontane, the most distinguished figure in the German novel of the Eighties and Nineties, had more to offer: a dryly realistic style, a benevolent irony, a flair for social nuances, understatement, and civilized conversation. An aristocrat by temperament, Fontane found the bourgeoisie problematic as well as comic. But what was Fontane compared to the Goncourts, Zola, or Tolstoi; what was Berlin to Paris or St. Petersburg?

Yet Mann's most immediate indebtedness was to less spectacular figures, to Scandinavian writers like Alexander Kielland and Jonas Lie, whose subject matter was allied to his own. Lübeck, as a Hanseatic city, was in a sense spiritually closer to the North than to Munich or Berlin; and since Ibsen, the Norwegians had enjoyed a great and often inflated reputation in the Reich. Lie and Kielland were both men of solid, unspectacular talent. The former's *The Family at Gilje* (1883), a novel dealing with the middle class, concerns itself largely with the lot of women who have to make marriages of convenience; the frustrated love between Inger-Johanna and the student Grip, a somewhat advanced and unconventional person, may have served as a model for the far more moving idyll between Toni Buddenbrook and Morten Schwarzkopf. Lie's genre pictures, the Christmas scene at Gilje, for instance, may have given Mann some useful hints, but one should not overstress the value to Mann of this rather undistinguished book. Alexander Kielland had more to offer. He was an elegant, cultivated, and rather complicated figure, who combined naturalistic seriousness with irony and self-irony, and democratic tendencies with pride in

34

his upper-class background. "He had himself sprung from one of these rich ship-owning, patrician families . . ." and it seems clear that Mann must have felt a considerable affinity with him. The "Hanseatic" side of Kielland is obvious in his *Garman and Worse* (1880), which might well have been subtitled "Decline of a Family" or "Decay of a Shipping Firm." His short stories, like Mann's, show a double heritage: the *Novelletter* (1879—translated as *Tales of Two Countries* in 1891) are located partly in Norway, partly in Paris. The protagonists in *Two Friends*, a novella of the love-hatred between a responsible burgher and a ne'er-do-well, afford a certain parallel to Thomas and Christian Buddenbrook.

The analogy between *Buddenbrooks* and Zola's *Rougon Macquart*, "Histoire d'une famille sous l'Empire," has been noted; and surely Mann's novel would have been very different—less solid, detailed, and documented—without the French precedent. There is no reason to question Mann's statement that he had not read Zola at the time he was composing *Buddenbrooks;* it was not necessary— Zola was in the air. (It was M. G. Conrad, one of Zola's major followers in Germany, who had published Mann's first novella in his *Die Gesellschaft*, a leading naturalistic journal.)

Yet Mann's debt to the "more artistic" Goncourt brothers was greater as well as more direct. For all of its naturalistic touches, *Buddenbrooks* is not intended as a "slice of life," but as a carefully arranged composition. Mann read *Renée Mauperin*, he tells us, "again and again, with delight in its lightness, successful execution, and precision . . . ," with "admiration which became productive." As originally planned, *Buddenbrooks* was to have been in scope and in manner much closer to the examples of the Goncourts than was the book that was actually written: a tightly organized novel of barely three hundred pages, centered on the last two generations. Something intervened. Mann speaks of the sheer mass of material furnished by a faithful Lübeck friend. More fundamental no doubt were his characteristic desire to get at the bottom of things, to go back as far as possible behind the coulisses of time, and his equally characteristic conviction that "only the thorough is truly interesting." This was not the only time in Mann's career that a relatively modest plan was to eventuate in a monumental book; the work, as he put it, showed a will of its own. *The Magic Mountain* and *Joseph* were to be even more strikingly transformed in the process of composition.

To return to the Goncourts—Mann intended, at one point, to emulate even their process of fraternal collaboration; his brother Heinrich was to take over the historical aspects of the novel. This notion was of course abandoned, but *Renée Mauperin* did provide insights into middle-class psychology which proved really useful, in its stress on the "reign of money," on business "ideals"—one thinks of the "practical ideals" of the second Johann Buddenbrook—and on the pride of bourgeois families. The skilfully distressing account of the heroine's prolonged illness may have strengthened Mann's inclination to treat scenes of disease, death, and decay.

Mann's debt to Tolstoi is more difficult to describe. He has testified that *Anna Karenina* "strengthened" him while he was writing *Buddenbrooks*. It would be difficult to think of two novels more different in spirit; very likely it was precisely the dissimilarity of the Russian work which he found helpful. Mr. André von Gronicka has argued that Mann learned the technique of the leitmotif in part from Tolstoi through Merezhkovski. Aside from this point, it is not tangible "influences" that are important here; one may speak rather of a certain affinity in Mann to Tolstoi's epic breadth and unhurried pace, of another "admiration which became productive."

To deal with the fortunes of four generations of Buddenbrooks, Mann found that he needed over seven hundred pages, divided among a host of chapters which are organized into eleven parts. For all its bulk, the novel has structure: the prestige and power of the family rise, reach a sort of plateau, and then imperceptibly slip into a decline which gradually gathers a terrifying momentum. It is Thomas, the central figure of the third generation, on whom the welfare of the family comes essentially to depend, so that the crisis of his life is also the crisis of the novel. The failures of his brother and sister, both obvious by the center of the work, isolate him increasingly, and the slow erosion of his strength makes inevitable the fall of the whole group.

This group does not exist in a vacuum; Mann shows its life against the background of the city-state of Lübeck, in whose oligarchic government the Buddenbrooks play a considerable role. Farther in the background, we are aware of the evolution of Germany from 1835 to about 1878: the emergence of German unity, prosperity, and material power as reflected in the customs union among the German states, the victorious Prussian wars with

Denmark, Austria, and France, and the sharp rise of commerce and trade. The broader developments are briefly mentioned without didactic digressions; the focus is always upon the Buddenbrooks as a particular group of very special individuals. Mann did not intend to write a symbolic novel of the German middle class, which was rising to new heights of prosperity during the period he describes, but rather to represent the decline of cultivated patricians, pushed to the wall by the new bourgeoisie. The testimony of his brother Viktor shows how Mann "stylized" the history of his family to heighten the impression of decadence. Yet the European reaction to *Buddenbrooks* suggests that his interpretation was by no means a merely arbitrary one but illuminated a very real social process.

Buddenbrooks is a novel of tradition as well as of decadence; the one implies the other. For the tradition of the patrician burgher, quite different from that of the "ordinary" middle class, Mann has profound respect. It stands for activity, energy, a degree of cultivation, and certain not too rigorous ethical standards, for "life" in a good sense. Despite ironic indications—fewer than one would expect—that the burgher's devotion to money is extreme, Mann is clearly on his side. There is no implication that the Buddenbrooks have amassed an undue amount of wealth; on the contrary, when the family bank balance sinks, we feel that the world is out of joint. Before their decline begins, the Buddenbrooks accept the business world in a robust, unquestioning way. Only in the third generation, with Thomas, do they become too delicate for the ethics of competition; only the sick Buddenbrook questions a *laissez-faire* capitalism. (Thomas, after a business reversal, perceives that his "best friends" react not with sympathy but with frigid distrust; he is weary and sensitive enough to consider this a personal injury.) Before that point, the Darwinian struggle for survival is taken as a matter of course. Not that the Buddenbrooks are Nietzschean buccaneers. "My son, engage joyfully in business during the day, but make only such deals that we can sleep well at night" is their motto—a very bourgeois code, but still a code. Without hypocrisy, one must be deeply concerned in preserving the appearance of solidity and respectability. Bankruptcy is the unforgivable sin. Thomas' feckless brother, Christian, can be excused for his failures, his sexual divagations, even his idleness; but when he remarks that every businessman is "really a swindler," no pardon is possible; his brother, a person by no means given to melodramatic gestures, is driven to pronounce a downright curse on him. The ideal Buddenbrook is a non-religious churchgoer whose ethic might have served as an instance of the inner bond between Protestantism and capitalism argued by Max Weber and Tawney. Religious fervor is suspect—it is not "solid"—music is still more so, and Thomas' taste for French novels and habit of citing Heine are clearly indications of danger.

Occasionally, Mann does treat his worthy patricians ironically, as in the repeated accounts of their fabulous meals, but his identification with them is too close to allow him to depart often from the tone of respect. His most ironic pages deal with the liberal bourgeoisie and the hopelessly docile working class. Thus the young student, Morten Schwarzkopf, believes ardently in the ideals of the ill-fated German liberal revolt of 1848—abolition of class distinctions, academic freedom, freedom of the press, and all the rest. He is a charming fellow, but clearly naive; we cannot take him seriously. When the "revolution" breaks out in Lübeck, the novel enters the realm of farce. The "people" break a few windows, demonstrate aimlessly for some hours, and then are sent home in good humor after some friendly words of paternal advice by the younger Johann Buddenbrook. Undoubtedly this account has a good deal of historical validity. One is reminded of Trotzky's remark that the German workers would not seize a railway station unless they had bought tickets first. In any case Mann's personal sympathies are clearly with the conservative side, where they remained until after the defeat of 1918.

Yet despite this affectionate respect for the patrician tradition, the theme of decadence clearly predominates. Decay is considered as an inevitable spiritual and biological process, not as an occasion of moral reproach. It is most strikingly shown in the succession of four male Buddenbrooks, three of whom are heads of the ancestral firm. Johann Buddenbrook, Sr. is a type of the eighteenth century as popularly conceived—rationalistic, optimistic, skeptical, and of uncomplicated, single-minded energy. His son, the younger Johann, is an excellent businessman and devoted to money; but his sentimental religiosity causes a split in his nature which leads to unconscious hypocrisy and "practical ideals." The Buddenbrooks are on the way to becoming problematic. With Thomas Buddenbrook they have become so. Thomas is the most appealing and impressive of the line. Cultivated, able, and enormously conscientious, he guides the family to its greatest successes, but he has no real belief in the value of his enterprises; his energies are eaten away.

Despite all his efforts, he cannot overcome the somehow innate tendency to dissolution which has overtaken the family like a sort of fate. At one point (VIII, 4) * he violates the traditional ethics of the firm in a desperate effort to recoup its fortunes, but the manoeuvre fails. After long and bitter struggles, he is utterly defeated. Yet his prolonged endeavor gives him stature: he has much of that "heroism of weakness" which Mann so greatly admires, and which he was to represent later in the more impressive figures of Schiller, in *A Weary Hour,* and of Gustave von Aschenbach. In Aristotelian terms, Thomas' flaw may be said to lie in his externality, evident in his sacrifice of human values to the welfare of the firm, and in his supreme concern for maintaining appearances. As his vitality decreases, he is forced more and more to mask his actual condition. Only Hanno, the most sensitive of the family, fully perceives this.

Shortly before his death, Thomas has an experience which could have saved him, spiritually speaking, but he lacks the force and courage to hold it in his grasp. More or less by chance he comes upon a volume of Schopenhauer and finds in it a source of metaphysical ecstasy. His cares suddenly appear unspeakably petty and indeed irrelevant; his own individuality and even that of his son seem unimportant.

> Have I hoped to live on in my son? In a personality yet more feeble, flickering, and timorous than my own? Blind, childish folly! What can my son do for me—what need have I of a son?

* References to *Buddenbrooks* are to part and chapter.

> Where shall I be when I am dead? Ah, it is so brilliantly clear, so overwhelmingly simple! I shall be in all those who have ever, do ever, or ever shall say "I"—*especially, however, in all those who say it most fully, potently, and gladly!*
>
> (X, 5)

Schopenhauer—or better, Schopenhauer modified by Nietzsche—could then have freed him from the tortures inflicted by the will. But he lacks the intellectual energy to maintain himself on these philosophical heights. He never opens the book again. One feels that this failure, like the others, is due less to any tangible defect in Thomas than to that inner weariness which, Mann implies, must be taken as given and lies beyond explanation.

Mann has made no secret of the fact that he has attributed to his not very intellectual hero a metaphysical experience of his own. One admires all the more the tact and skill which make the episode credible, and the control which keeps ideology in its place. *Buddenbrooks,* in this regard, is more of a work of art than most of the later novels.

While Thomas, in his way, is a tragic figure, his son Hanno is pathetic. He is possessed of some musical talent but lacks the strength for any sort of career, let alone that of restoring the shaken fortunes of the family. He is phenomenally sickly, and dies while still a schoolboy, physically of sickness but essentially of decadence. With him the family comes to an end. The theme of successive and cumulative decline is repeated in a number of lesser figures.

What happens to the Buddenbrooks is a decline only from the point of view of normality. As always, Mann shows the opposite aspect: in terms of "the spirit" the process is one of ascent to greater awareness and intellectuality, to art, and to—death. Life and the spirit are irreconcilable foes; there is no hope, in Mann's early thought, of a possible synthesis, and the suggestion of a possible *juste milieu* would have been rejected as childishly optimistic. Mann clearly implies in *Buddenbrooks* that the game of the spirit is not worth the candle. Not until *Tonio Kröger* does he reach a rather wry acceptance of the life and the role of the a-normal, artistic person.

Decadence then is inevitable and has a potentially creative aspect, but it is greatly to be feared. Mann devotes all his powers of naturalistic description and all his psychological subtlety to develop the theme. It is with the sentimental religiosity of the younger Johann Buddenbrook that feelings "other than the normal, every-day sentiments proper to good citizens" enter the family tradition and begin to alienate it from life. From this point, early in the novel, until the horrible death of the adolescent Hanno, the process takes its inexorable course. (At times Mann implies a dubious biology: decay would seem to be in the blood.) Largely it is seen as a physical development: all the later Buddenbrooks are labile, they tend to migraines, carious teeth, premature aging, and "bluish shadows below the eyes." The terms "nervous" and "exhausted" occur again and again. But primarily the evolution is psychological: with greater self-consciousness come extreme subjectivity and introversion. Energy, and finally the will to live itself, fall away; it is Hanno's lack of *élan vital* that makes him succumb to typhus. In him, as earlier in Christian, the "death wish" becomes dominant. Loy-

alty to the family and the firm gradually becomes a problem, and then an insoluble one. Artistic, and above all
musical endowment is not merely a symptom of the decline; it is a causal factor. Christian, the artist *manqué*,
is merely grotesque, but Gerda and her son Hanno are
mortally threatened. In Gerda's affair with Lieutenant
von Throta, music is linked, as so often in Mann, to illicit
love; for Hanno, it is his chief solace, but also his greatest
danger. The cumulative effect of the workings of the
forces of decay is such that one welcomes Hanno's death
as a release too long withheld.

Looking back on the novel, we realize with what careful persistence Mann has developed the theme of death
as a force possessed of an uncanny fascination. This note
is first sounded briefly, without apparent emphasis, during
the last illness of the wife of the elder Johann Buddenbrook. "Something new, alien, extraordinary seemed to
have entered the house, a secret which they read in each
other's eyes; the thought of death had gained admission
and ruled silently . . ." It is struck again and again, with
increasing frequency and force. Schopenhauer makes
death seem a boon to Thomas in his worst days; and Hanno's boyhood is so filled with funerals that it is almost
an education for dying. The smell of death, "the alien
and yet so familiar odor," repels and yet attracts him, as
it was later to attract Hans Castorp.

That death should play a part of central importance in
a story of decline is hardly surprising, but Mann elaborates
on the theme in a way which goes far beyond what the
inherent logic of the situation or the tenets of naturalism

could demand. It becomes increasingly obvious that he found death (or what the Germans curiously call the "problem" of death) more important, more interesting, more germane to his talents than life. It is here above all that he appears as the heir of German romanticism. Not that he indulges in any facile raptures; he is far too much the conscientious observer for that. One needs to recall only the famous chapter on typhus (XI, 3), or the picture of Thomas Buddenbrook after his collapse on the street:

> Since the street sloped sharply downwards, the upper part of his body was quite a bit lower than his feet. He had fallen on his face, from under which a pool of blood at once began to spread out. His hat rolled down a way on the road. His fur coat was spattered with filth and melting snow. His hands, in their white kid gloves, lay outstretched in a puddle. (X, 7)

As the novel of the eighteenth century tended to end in a marriage or series of marriages, *Buddenbrooks* draws to its close in a succession of deaths. At the beginning of the last section, four minor characters are dispatched on a single page. (XI, 1) The development of the theme reaches its climax in the chapter which recounts Hanno's death of typhus. This follows immediately, with all the shock of suddenness, upon an ironic, in part almost comic account of Hanno's day at the *Gymnasium*. "A case of typhus takes the following course." Picturing the disease as a general force strengthens its impact by making its power more impersonal, greater, and more ghastly. Mann withholds no clinical detail, but he has given these pages an eloquence and rhythm of their own. Hanno's illness is transformed into a drama; the crisis is dramatic as well as medical; and it is a psychological force, not the illness as such, that prevails.

The account of the onset of typhus is one of the high points of German naturalism, and it is only one of many passages in *Buddenbrooks* which demonstrate that Mann had little more to learn about exact observation and description. Whether or not the story that Mann once scrutinized a departing friend through opera glasses is true, it is highly credible; when one reads that Grünlich had put "a little powder on the wart on the left side of his nose" on the day of his wedding with Toni Buddenbrook (III, 14), one thinks of Zeiss glasses and telescopic lenses. Permaneder, who succeeds him in Toni's affections, is described (VI, 4) with equal accuracy but less malice. One notes also, especially in the first part, the careful documentation to give historical flavor. Mann's method is phonographic as well as photographic, employing Bavarian dialect as well as *Plattdeutsch*, and reproducing even the curiously modified vowels of Sesemi Weichbrodt's dialect.

But there is much more here than naturalistic reproduction. As so often, Mann displays his flair for giving the effect of a musical work; above all in his account of Hanno's composition. (VIII, 6)

Soft and clear as a bell sounded the E-minor chord, tremolo pianissimo, amid the purling, flowing notes of the violin. It swelled, it broadened, it slowly, slowly rose: suddenly, in the forte, he introduced the discord C-sharp, which led back to the original key, and the Stradivarius ornamented it with its welling and singing. He dwelt on the dissonance until it became fortissimo. But he denied himself and his audience the resolution; he kept it back. What would it be, this resolution, this enchanting, satisfying absorption into the B-major chord? A joy beyond compare, a gratification of overpowering sweetness! Peace! Bliss! The kingdom of Heaven: only not yet—not yet! A moment more of striving, hesitation, suspense, that must become well-nigh intolerable in order to heighten the ultimate moment of joy.

His use of light and his feeling for subtle gradations of color as well as for brilliance, relate him closely to the impressionist school. Thus, in description of a warm January day:

> The pavement was wet and dirty, and snow was dripping from the gray gables. But above them the sky stretched delicate blue and unmarred, and billions of atoms of light seemed to glitter like crystals in the azure and to dance. (X, 7)

The scene around the Buddenbrooks' Christmas tree (VIII, 8) is a Manet in words: the whole picture is constructed of a multitude of lights—the countless flames of little candles, the larger lights, the reflections. Mann is equally successful with softer tones, as in this sentence describing an interior just before a storm.

> The colors in the room, the tones of the landscapes on the walls, the yellow of the furniture and the curtains had faded, one could no longer see the play of nuances in Toni's dress or the brightness in people's eyes. (IV, 11)

The leitmotif is employed prodigally in *Buddenbrooks,* and put to a variety of uses, from the rather trivial to the broadly symbolic. It can emphasize a purely physical characteristic, like Toni's "somewhat prominent upper lip" or Gerda's dark-red hair. More importantly, it can pick out a physical trait which has psychological significance:

47

Tom's nervousness, either explicitly stated or implied by repeated mention of his Russian cigarettes; or the bluish shadows below Gerda's eyes. The extension of such a motif from one character to another of course establishes a bond between the two: thus Toni later shares in Tom's nervousness, and Hanno "inherits" his mother's bluish shadows. (That he possesses this sign of weariness at the age of four weeks [VII, 1] would seem to be an instance of the triumph of theory over artistic judgment.)

A repeated word or phrase can of course characterize the speaker: thus the insuperably childish Toni never outgrows the word *vornehm* (upper-class; "Ritzy"); or a motif can be used with humorous intent or for a dozen other purposes. It is most successfully employed, however, as a device of reminiscence; this sort of leitmotif can call up a whole cluster of associations and psychological subtleties. To have its full, "musical" value, the associations evoked must be emotionally charged; the motif with purely descriptive or ironic intent, like "who associated with the best families," has a far less powerful appeal, and its repeated use tends more easily to tire the reader. Broadly speaking, the motifs of *Buddenbrooks* do not have as much emotional content, so to speak, as those of later works, notably *Tonio Kröger* and *The Magic Mountain*. There is one very striking exception: the phrase "to sit on the stones," ultraprosaic though it seems, is used both subtly and movingly. Toni's first lover had been obliged to sit on a pile of stones while she chatted with upper-class friends; then the phrase came to mean, to the two of them, "to be neglected and lonely"; after giving up her lover, Toni uses the phrase again and again, in all

sorts of contexts, sometimes without herself remember-
ing, apparently, the whole richness of association. But the
alert reader does remember, and the five words revivify
a whole series of recollections, causing the story of Toni
to "be all there in a given moment."

This economy of means, which makes the leitmotif a
sort of shorthand for the emotions, is perhaps its chief
merit. When used too often, as occasionally towards the
end of *Buddenbrooks,* the device can very easily become
as boring as an old family joke.

The manipulation of a variety of other techniques shows
how far from the novel of naturalism *Buddenbrooks* really
is. For example, the use of contrast: after telling of a particularly depressing incident in the life of Thomas Buddenbrook, Mann shifts quickly to the music of Bach; it
is no accident that the discussion centers on counterpoint.
(VIII, 6) A similar contrapuntal effect is produced by the
introduction of the Christmas festival as a pleasant interlude within the sordid story of Herr Weinschenk's troubles
with the law. (VIII, 8) Musical also is the effect of acceleration gained at the end through the rapidly repeated
blows of death and disaster and the accumulation of the
evidences of decay. Probably Mann gives us too much of
a good thing—that the Buddenbrooks' dentist, for instance,
is decadent too would seem to be a clear case of piling
Ossa on Pelion; it may be that the influence of Wagner
has something to do with this tendency towards excess.
Possibly Mann's later device, so notable in *Joseph,* of
repeating a whole incident, or introducing, under another name, a character who is "archetypically" the same
as one who has preceded him, is foreshadowed in his first

novel. Thus Toni's first husband, Grünlich, turns out to be a swindler, and the marriage ends in divorce; her daughter Erika goes through fundamentally the same experience with Hugo Weinschenk.

Buddenbrooks is an end and a beginning. After writing incomparably the best of German "family novels" Mann abandoned the genre, and never again was he to come so close to the pure epic. *Buddenbrooks* is obviously the least problematic and complex of his major works, but it is not without its paradoxes: realistic in manner, it is romantic in spirit; abundant in Dickensian *Gemütlichkeit*, its essence is the mood of "the cross, death, and the grave"; apparently unilinear in its treatment of time, it uses the leitmotif on occasion to give the effect of emotional simultaneity. From the perspective of our own day, one can see how the technical innovations of the novel point forward to more experimental works to come.

4. NARCISSUS

IN THE FIRST DECADE OF THE CENTURY, MANN'S CONCERN
with the artist increased, reaching a degree which threatened, for some years, to make him a very specialized writer
indeed. That he was fascinated by the "problem" of artist
and burgher was less narrowing than the circumstance of
obsession with himself, for the two polar types are fundamentally only the two sides of his own personality. This
extreme introspection restricted the breadth, but did not
of course impair the intrinsic quality of Mann's work;
Death in Venice, both in psychological penetration and
in style, is unequaled among his shorter narratives. Yet
self-portraiture, even of the most engaging and complex
self, has obvious limitations. The time comes when the
vein begins to be exhausted.

The most representative and distinguished stories of
the period are, as expressions of the self, essentially lyric.
When, after the time of relative sterility which followed
Death in Venice, Mann again produced work of the first

51

rank, it was with a partial return to the epic, in *The Magic Mountain.* Not that he has ever renounced the theme of the artist, self-portraiture, or subjectivity, but the "non-ego" is accorded a renewed importance, the balance is redressed. And even in his most introspective works he had preserved exactness of eye and precision of style.

The protagonist of *The Hungry* (1902), a lonely intellectual, reaches the conclusion that he is as hungry and pitiable as the tramp whom he meets on a wintry night. This bathetic little piece is important mainly because of its relation to *Tonio Kröger:* Mann "cannibalized" it, taking over its more memorable formulations into that novella, which appeared in the following year.

Tonio Kröger is Mann's most lyrical story. As a direct *apologia,* it is warmer in tone than the earlier stories. Mann is closer to autobiography here than ever before, and sympathy with Tonio, and a pity approaching self-pity, are not restrained.

Tonio Kröger is a writer of great talents, though he finds production a slow, unrelenting torment. But it is primarily the basic condition of his existence from which he suffers: he is doubly isolated. He has escaped from the world of his paternal tradition, but he is no more at home among the Bohemians of Munich than he had been among the burghers, and the latter he had at least respected. Either to resolve his dilemma, or at least to find a means of making it bearable and fruitful, is the "problem" of Tonio's existence. He himself prefers to put it more grandiloquently, in terms of the eternal and irreconcilable conflict between "spirit" and "life."

In part, no doubt, Tonio is the victim of his own ideol-

ogy. The "spirit" (including of course art and the intellect) is conceived of as dead, while "life" is basically bourgeois and banal. Once one has escaped from the fascination of Mann's language, one realizes that his great antithesis is after all only a very arbitrary one. But to Tonio this extreme dualism reveals the essence of the universe; it is small wonder that he finds his existence "a bit hard," as he says with studied understatement. If one accepts the assumption that "the artist" is necessarily and eternally cut off from all vitality and human warmth, then the masochistic analogies Tonio draws between the artist and the outcast or the eunuch are sound. "And if I, I all alone, had achieved the Nine Symphonies, *The World as Will and Representation* and the "Last Judgment," you would be eternally right in laughing at me," he exclaims (in thought) to a blonde young lady. Any "normal" person is superior to Beethoven, Schopenhauer, and Michelangelo —this is the "treason of the intellectuals" with a vengeance. Coming from Tonio, the sentiment is understandable, and it is a tribute to Mann's skill that one does not immediately realize its enormous absurdity. But even Tonio cannot really believe it.

To turn from these abstractions to the work itself: *Tonio Kröger* is clearly and symmetrically constructed. The first pages develop Tonio's sense of isolation and inferiority, largely by the vivid account of his unreciprocated feelings for Hans Hansen and Ingeborg Holm, the exemplars of the seductive beauty of normality. (They are blond, he is not; this note is heard again and again.) The growing consciousness of his gifts as a writer only cuts him off the more from the world of "life." He flees from

53

this milieu, though he never completely rejects it psychologically; he is plagued by the sense of apostasy from the traditions of his father. Lisaveta Ivanovna, his confidante, makes him recognize his true position for the first time. He is a bourgeois after all, but a "lost burgher," a "Bohemian with a bad conscience." This insight, strategically placed in the center of the novella, is its turning point. In search of further self-knowledge, Tonio returns to the North. After an ironic interlude in his native city he experiences, in Denmark, what Joyce would have called an epiphany. Hans Hansen and Ingeborg Holm return, not in person but as types; again he is overwhelmed by their beauty and unproblematic self-sufficiency. But by now he has come to accept his own position: it is precisely his frustrated love for the Nordic-normal-bourgeois which gives him the inner tension that makes him creative. Henceforth he will try neither to identify himself with the Bohemian nor to seduce the burgher into the realm of art. He will stand between, a sympathetic if ironic mediator. In a letter to Lisaveta which forms the ending of the story, he draws the balance of his existence:

> I gaze into an unborn and shadowy world, which needs to be given order and form; I see a throng of shadows of human figures, who beckon to me that I weave spells to redeem them: tragic and ridiculous figures, and those that are both at the same time—and to these last I am much devoted. But my deepest and most secret love belongs to the blond and blue-eyed, the clear, vital ones, the happy, lovable, and commonplace.
>
> Do not find fault with this love, Lisaveta; it is good and fruitful. There is longing in it and melancholy envy and the least trace of scorn and a complete, chaste bliss.

These last lines of Tonio Kröger remind one of the magnificent ending of *A Portrait of the Artist as a Young Man.* Mann's lyrical novella occupies a place in his development similar to that of Joyce's pedagogical novel within his work. Both Tonio and Stephen Dedalus come to accept the role of the artist; each has a sense of mission; each gives a programmatic statement of his ambitions. Yet in Dedalus' words:

> Welcome, O life! I go to encounter for the millionth time the reality of experience and to forge in the smithy of my soul the uncreated conscience of my race.

there is a fanfare of trumpets, a determination which makes one aware of a certain softness and sentimentality in Mann's protagonist. Tonio, no doubt, would have found such youthful exuberance naive. In his most positive affirmation an elegiac note remains. The strength, the sense of activity of Joyce's passage lie beyond the grasp of Mann's gentler and somewhat narcissistic hero. In Gustave von Aschenbach he was to portray an artist of more heroic stamp.

In *Tonio Kröger,* Mann uses the leitmotif more abundantly and in a more "musical" manner than in any previous work. It has among others a structural function: the whole action is held together by the motifs which bind a late passage to an early one. For example, as a boy Tonio expresses his pride in his family and his middle-class conscience in the words: "We are no gypsies in a green wagon"; when it recurs later, the phrase draws the whole passage associated with it back into close contact with what has gone before; and the entire novella gains in solidity. The sense of recognition and reminiscence is such that Tonio almost literally relives his own past. Repetition is not limited to words and phrases; that Hans and Inge or the dancing of the quadrille "recur" is a natural extension.

Above all, the motifs seem to have been chosen to produce nostalgia and loneliness, almost as if they had been borrowed from lyrics by Heine or Storm. Thus the wild-flower in his father's buttonhole, and the "old walnut tree," always linked with a fountain and the sea. The effect of melancholy isolation is increased by weaving in references to Hamlet (whom the Germans generally romanticize), to Schiller's *Don Carlos,* and to a poem of Storm's. Mann once implied that *Tonio Kröger* was the work most peculiarly his own, and its warm, personal, somehow youthful quality explains in part its vast popular appeal. It is, if the paradox is allowable, a sentimental masterpiece.

The hero of *A Weary Hour* (1905) is made of sterner stuff. This brief work, written in celebration of the centenary of Schiller's death, is a study of the artist in Schiller's mask rather than an attempt at an "objective" essay, as Mann has indicated by grouping it with his novellas. It is essentially a reproduction of the poet's self-doubts during an hour when he has lost faith in his own talents, set in a form which approaches the interior monologue. Like Aschenbach, Mann's Schiller is a believer in the ethics of achievement; like Tonio Kröger, he finds production a torment. Yet he holds that the pain of writing is the seal of its quality and is determined that his sufferings must not have been in vain. Knowing that he is mortally ill, he is committed to creation as a desperate "nevertheless." He is in other words a symbol of Mann's new ideal of himself. The artist is no longer a sort of charlatan; he is like Dürer's knight who presses forward "despite death and the devil." The study, primarily symbolic in intent, aims also to recreate the historical Schiller. The poet's incandescent ambition, his need—rather ironically recorded —to use "big and beautiful words" to explain the conditions of his life, and his "yearning hostility" towards his greater rival, Goethe, all contribute to a convincing and touching portrait.

Royal Highness (1909) is Mann's first attempt at a light novel; it is fundamentally a transposition of his usual themes into the realm of comedy, or better, of fairy tale. Light though the work is, it is unabashedly didactic. Its basic assumptions are amazingly optimistic: decadence can be overcome, isolation and its handicaps are to be taken as spurs to distinction, a synthesis of life and art, content and form, the twentieth century and the aristocratic principle, can be reached. The novel, in its exuberant happiness, reflects Mann's courtship and recent marriage; it too is a part of his symbolic biography.

An optimistic book, *Royal Highness* springs from an optimistic tradition. Mann turned here to the *Bildungsroman*, the genre which traces the education of an individual towards a harmonious development of all his powers. As in Goethe's *Wilhelm Meister's Apprenticeship*, one follows the hero through a variety of experiences until he has attained a degree of maturity and "form" and is ready to play a part in the world. On his way, he has been exposed to a number of influences, and usually at least one person has consciously tried to guide him. In *Royal Highness* the pedagogue is Raoul Überbein; he is the forerunner of Naphta and Settembrini in that far richer novel of education, *The Magic Mountain*.

The young prince Klaus Heinrich, who bears the typical stigmata of the lonely hero, is called upon to play a role which is purely representative. He holds a rank in the army but knows nothing of war; he must read speeches, written by others, which he does not understand. To be sure, this purely formal existence has intrinsic value: the prince represents the *imago* of his people, serving as its idealized symbol of itself. Yet the inherent dangers of such a position become obvious in the devitalization and weariness which mark the lives of other members of the royal family. To avoid these, he must effect the reconciliation of form and life. Überbein, the poet Axel Martini, and even the collie Percy, who is not the least interesting of Mann's decadents, are confronted with similar problems.

Parallel to Klaus Heinrich's condition and in a large degree dependent on it is the situation of his country, an independent South German state which is a cross between Bavaria and a comic-opera kingdom. Mann has pictured the milieu with benevolent irony and elaborate detail: the court etiquette, the omnipresent titles, the decaying grandeurs of castles and official affairs. For the half-comic Grand Duchy has serious problems: organized on feudal principles, it must adjust itself to modern capitalism to survive.

In his half-conscious search for "real" life, Klaus Heinrich finds that there is no uncomplicated solution. He is not particularly aristocratic by nature, but he comes to accept the isolation of his position as necessary; humiliating experience and the precepts of Überbein teach him that a simple egalitarianism is false and sentimental. There must be "distance." Yet in large part the answer comes, literally and symbolically, from America: a German-American heroine refuses to accept Klaus Heinrich until he has broken out of his formal existence to some grasp of reality (in this case, of economics); her father, a fabulous multi-millionaire, then finances and saves the state. The American principle is seen as a sort of social and economic modernism, a coming to terms with the new age, an overcoming of certain prejudices—the prince marries a commoner. But to the extent that this "didactic fairy tale," as Hermann Bahr called it, is political in its intention, it teaches a rationalized aristocracy, not democracy. The American "dollar princess" becomes a Royal Highness too. Love has released the prince from isolation, but even love must be combined with "distance" and dignity. "That shall be our life from now on: both, majesty and love—a severe happiness" is Klaus Heinrich's final formulation.

As one would expect, the aesthetic "moral" of the story is more important than the socio-political; it is a mirror for artists rather than for princes. For Klaus Heinrich's existence, made up of a series of symbolic actions, is of course an analogue of the artist's, more particularly of the actor's. He must stay on his side of the footlights, a bit remote from the audience, but he must have a real bond with life or he is lost as a human being. His "severe happiness" is the expression of an ideal more resolute than Tonio Kröger's, more human than Aschenbach's.

The objection that *Royal Highness* smacks too much of the success story and the happy ending is largely irrelevant. The atmosphere of the fairy tale, established by such devices as the prophecy of the gypsy woman, the rose bush which regains its fragrance on a day of public rejoicing, and so on, should warn us not to take things too literally. If *Royal Highness*, diverting and charming though it is, is not one of Mann's real successes, the reason lies in a discrepancy between ends and means, between the machinery of a light novel and a rather heavy weight of didactic intention.

No such discrepancy mars *Felix Krull*, which Mann took up after finishing *Royal Highness*. A fragment of *Felix Krull* appeared in 1911; sections in 1924 and 1937; the completed first volume was published in 1954. It is discussed more fully below; a few sentences here should show the place of the early Krull in Mann's gallery of portraits. Though he reverts here to the concept of the artist as mountebank, he is no longer disturbed by the equation: Felix, true to his name, recounts his career with cheerful amorality. His evasion of military service by performing a carefully rehearsed epileptic fit before a draft board, is Mann's best comic scene. Throughout the rather elaborate depiction of Krull, all heaviness is neatly avoided. He relates his education for crime with a delicious sanctimoniousness, and believes, not without reason, that he is "carved of finer wood" than his dull (and honest) contemporaries; he sees his whole life as a work of art. Mann, who has described his own relation towards the German cultural tradition as both affectionate and dissolvent, has successfully parodied the Goethean ideal of conscious self-education, and made his hero speak in a stately prose which recalls *Poetry and Truth* and *Wilhelm Meister.*

From birth, Krull's development is that of the artist: his imagination, his flair for assuming a role, his narcissism, his great love of the glories of this world, all appear as representative and yet individual. His first theft, a successful *aesthetic* experience, gives him the same sensation as did his erotic day dreams. Not the least of his achievements is the rich-textured prose style in which his memoirs are set.

It is a measure of Mann's complexity that he turned from *Felix Krull* to *Death in Venice* (1911): the most heroic portrait of the artist follows directly after the most scurrilous. In Gustave von Aschenbach, Mann represented, in a highly stylized way, his own image of himself, his achievements and ambitions, and his new concept of the writer as intellectual guide and ethical model for a whole generation. The novella is also an expression of a gnawing anxiety about the cost, in human terms, of playing the role of the "hero of creative work."

For Aschenbach, who exemplifies his own precept that weariness may be overcome by a supreme exertion of the will, is ripe for disaster. To his contemporaries he is the conqueror of decadence, but he is also secretly its victim. His career has been built by forcing and overstraining his talent, repeatedly and victoriously. Too great a devotion to the Prussian ideals of duty and discipline brings him to the point of collapse; the "death wish" rebels against the categorical imperative of his conscious mind.

Aschenbach, before his fall, has risen to splendid heights. Frail and nervous in constitution, he has produced works, ranging from the psychological narrative through the novel of ideas to the critical essay, in which Mann's own projects seem to be reflected. Like Tonio Kröger, he had "revealed the mysteries, cast suspicions on genius, betrayed art" in his problematic youth, but in his maturity he has assumed a representative and dignified role. His own talent, like Mann's, is "equally far removed from the banal and the eccentric, constituted to win both the confidence of the broad public and the admiring, stimulating interest of the fastidious." Mann has linked him with a succession of determined ascetics— with Frederick the Great, Savonarola, Schiller, and with his favorite symbol of triumphant suffering, Saint Sebastian.

This strange mixture of Prussian and artist is called by a mysterious messenger to Venice, for Mann as for many others the "romantic city *par excellence*" and as such the city of death. Venice is suffused, for the German public, with a special richness of reminiscence: it is associated with the poet Platen, with Nietzsche, and with Wagner, who died there. Evocations of antiquity in the novella, like the use of dactylic lines which approach the hexameter, emphasize that Aschenbach is fleeing from the harsh German world to the classic Mediterranean; but his Italian journey comes too late to save him. After his encounter with the boy Tadzio, the allusions to Plato and to Hellenistic sculpture establish the mood for his homosexual passion.

Death in Venice is even more carefully wrought than

Tonio Kröger. As Vernon Venable has shown, its symbolism is both elaborate and carefully controlled. A series of sinister figures, all related to the "messenger" who appears at the beginning of the story, serves both to warn Aschenbach and to entice him to his doom. The "Charon" who takes him to the Lido in a gondola is the most uncanny of them. It is typical of Mann's dualism that the important symbols have diametrically opposed significances: thus the jungle, the source of the plague which attacks Venice, signifies rank fertility as well as death; and Tadzio, the occasion of Aschenbach's degradation, is also, as an incorporation of the symbol of Saint Sebastian, an incarnation of his art.

Like the mature Aschenbach, Mann has "banished every common word" from this novella. In this one story, he comes close to the cool monumentality of Stefan George; the style has a chiseled and deliberately stately quality.

Death in Venice conveys a sense of inevitability unique in Mann's work. One is not surprised to read, in his *Sketch of My Life,* that he had in writing it "a sovereign sense of being borne up" such as he had never experienced before. It is the least "bourgeois" of his works, at once consummately civilized and deeply barbaric. It gives a sense of the classical world in a way Mann equaled only in the vision of Greece in *The Magic Mountain,* while the savage frenzy of Aschenbach's dream of the jungle is unparalleled and unexpected in Mann. Finally, of course, it is the high point in his series of portraits of the artist. The coming of the War was soon to turn his interests in other directions, but it is hard to conceive that he could have surpassed this novella, under any conditions.

5. GERMANY AND EUROPE

BETWEEN *Death in Venice* (1911) AND *The Magic Mountain* (1924), Mann completed no major work of fiction. It is rather startling to find such a break in the production of so fertile and systematically industrious a novelist, but the reasons are not far to seek. Most obvious is the "thunder clap," the outbreak of the First World War, which called him from the enchanted mountain of aestheticism to the flatland of politics, a terrain in which he found himself, at first, grotesquely out of place. Like most German intellectuals, Mann instinctively took his position on the side of the Wilhelminian empire; unlike most of them, he found it necessary to take stock, to examine painstakingly the conservative, romantic, musical, anti-intellectual tradition which he identified with Germany. One of the immediate results of this self-examination was the long delay, and eventually the complete transformation of the literary project which finally resulted in *The Magic Mountain*. Mann had planned a brief, comic pendant to *Death in*

Venice, based on a three weeks' visit to Davos in 1912. Something like a more satiric *Tristan* might have emerged. But, under the impact of the War, Mann was impelled first to wrestle with all the "problems" which it evoked. His intellectual struggles, best understood as the attempt to reconcile the German position with his own conscience and his special position as an artist, are recorded in various essays of 1914–18, of which his *Frederick and the Great Coalition* (1915) is the most interesting. This is not a work of vulgar nationalistic hero-worship: Frederick II of Prussia emerges as a problematic character, a moral radical, who breaks with the ethical precepts of the West in the name of a higher necessity. He is a figure akin to Gustave von Aschenbach in his devotion to a task almost too great for his powers.

The most important of Mann's "war books" is his *Reflections of a Non-Political Man,* composed of a series of essays written during the War and published as a unit in 1918. "Compare yourself with others! Recognize who you are!" is one of the epigraphs of the volume, and Mann obeys this Goethean injunction with painful and almost embarrassing conscientiousness. It is a repetitious, confused, wordy book, marked by that pseudo-profundity to which German intellectuals so often incline when they discuss politics, and the reckless manipulation of such antitheses as culture and civilization, nature and "spirit." Central to the work is the notion that there is an irreconcilable opposition between German culture and "politics," which term Mann manages to equate with democracy and Western civilization. Always disciplined and professional as

65

an artist, Mann argues, in the *Reflections,* with the enthusiastic looseness of the autodidact.

Fortunately, it is unnecessary to discuss the book at length. In his *The German Republic,* which appeared only four years later, Mann repudiated its political views, and its major themes are treated with brilliance and detachment in *The Magic Mountain,* for which the volume of essays served as a sort of undress rehearsal. Yet even the *Reflections* has a place in Mann's development. The book contains sections of interesting literary criticism, above all of self-criticism. Its main value was clearly cathartic, purging him of reactionary nationalism. And the tension and vividness of much of the great debate between Settembrini and Naphta derive from the earlier debate, which runs through the *Reflections,* between Mann and his liberal, "Western" brother Heinrich. (It was at the same time a dispute between two sides of his own personality.) Finally, the impact of the War enlarged his intellectual horizon enormously: he became less narcissistic, less obsessed with his own image. Hans Castorp is, to be sure, an analogue of the artist, but he is primarily a German Everyman. Indeed, after *Death in Venice,* what more could Mann say about the artist as such? It is significant that the brilliant fragment *Felix Krull,* which equates creative talent with criminality, was not finished for so long a time.

The Magic Mountain

In a sense, *The Magic Mountain* is a symbolic record of Mann's development from Lübeck on: above all, of his fascination by decadence, illness, and death, in short by the ideas of German romanticism as he understood them, and of his eventual liberation from this fascination. It is not of course a literal record. The "simple" Hans Castorp represents the author only in a sharply limited way; and elements of Mann's personality and thought are expressed in other characters of the novel—in Naphta, in Clavdia Chauchat, even in the uncomplicated Joachim Ziemssen. *The Magic Mountain,* like most other great novels of education, draws heavily on the autobiographical.

Hans Castorp is, so to speak, a distant cousin of the Buddenbrooks and Tonio Kröger. He too comes from a wealthy and respected Hanseatic family with a strong sense of tradition; his early boyhood, like Hanno Buddenbrook's, has been overshadowed by death. Apparently, there is nothing remarkable about Castorp: he is of average gifts, conventional tastes, and thoroughly bourgeois inclinations. Yet in him is a "sympathy with death," a flair for disease and decay, which constitutes both his danger and his distinction. Illness, in Mann's dark lexicon, may be synonymous with intellect or even genius, and Castorp's latent tendency to tuberculosis is a sign of hidden talents.

In the course of Mann's skilfully delayed exposition, we become aware that the Castorp who goes to Davos "for three weeks" and stays seven years is by no means the agreeable nonentity that he at first appears. Before he is exposed to the concentrated education of the mountain, his personality has already been formed by certain primal experiences. In his admirable interpretation of *The Magic Mountain,* H. J. Weigand speaks of four:

67

continuity (the sense of tradition), death, freedom (a freedom from responsibility, which gives rise to a feeling of exhilaration mingled with shame), and Eros (his adolescent love for Pribislav Hippe.) One may add a fifth: the realization that the world about him was out of joint, that contemporary society offered no goals worthy of the activity of a thoughtful person. In this fifth experience particularly, Castorp is representative not only of the German burgher but of a whole European generation. The "flatland" is infested with disease as well as the mountain, and only by exposing oneself to the hermetically intensified illnesses of the sanatorium is there any hope of gaining a new health. Hans is to go through a process very like that of psychoanalysis: his ills, and by extension those of Europe, must be drawn clearly into consciousness before there can be any hope of recovery. But neither he nor the reader is aware, for a long time, that any such process is under way.

The Magic Mountain can be read on a number of levels: on a naive plane, as a realistic novel; as a myth of the young hero who goes on a journey, dallies with a seductress in a *Venusberg*, encounters dangers and adventures, and finally reaches his goal; as an allegory of Germany between East and West; or as a philosophical novel, in which the forces of reason and enlightenment battle with the romantic attractions of death, and both are at last combined in a grandiose if precarious synthesis. Clearly, each approach has its values. The latter two have been the most attractive to interpreters, since they can be closely related to Mann's own development as shown in the *Reflections* and elsewhere. Yet they involve the danger of treating *The Magic Mountain* as if it were a sort of bastard philosophy of history rather than a novel, while Mann's most astounding achievement was to transform the cloudy abstractions of his essays into people as vivid as Clavdia Chauchat or Joachim Ziemssen. Not that one can ignore the "ideas"; they give body and richness to the whole, but they form but one of the elements of the work of art. If one approaches *The Magic Mountain* in terms of the tradition to which it belongs, and which Mann consciously followed, that of the novel of education, it should be possible to keep realism and symbolism, human beings and ideas, in proper perspective. For the hero of the German *Bildungsroman* characteristically undergoes both emotional and intellectual adventures, and neither need be stressed at the expense of the other. The white arms of Clavdia Chauchat are at least as important to Castorp as the theories of Settembrini or the *Weltanschauung* of Peeperkorn; and Joachim Ziemssen is more valuable to him, and to us, as a human being than as a symbol of the Prussian ideal of duty. He is both, of course.

Castorp, the young man in search of an education, is exposed to an almost infinite variety of persons, ideas, and influences. Here Mann's pervasive irony has added a new dimension and a new difficulty to the novel. The traditional hero meets guides and tempters, but here no guide is to be completely trusted and no tempter may be wholly rejected. The mountain itself has a dual aspect: it is of course the realm of death and can be equated with the underworld or the grave, but precisely as such it offers the possibility of rebirth. Its hermetic isolation, again, has two very different implications. Apart from all the normal concerns of life, even from time and the succession of the seasons, it is the realm of freedom, in a negative sense: its inhabitants enjoy that release from responsibility which Castorp instinctively equates with shame. Yet this very hermetic quality makes it an unequaled if perilous place of education. Castorp's personality is intensified as in the retort of an alchemist; his heightened fever symbolizes the acceleration of all his faculties. Combining as it does danger and the possibility of renascence, the mountain is essentially a place of initiation. Settembrini's reference to *The Magic Flute* is highly relevant; one thinks of Masonic rites, and of far earlier ones as well.

It is the willingness of Castorp to take risks, to "die and be reborn," which raises him above mediocrity. That this adventurousness derives, in Mann's view, from his tendency to illness, hardly needs to be mentioned. Outwardly, he is phlegmatic and conventional, and nearly always he is passive; but he is open to adventure. In the "heightened" world of the mountain, he has courage, and only once, in the séance, does he find it necessary to retreat before an experience. "*Placet experiri*" is the first lesson he learns from Settembrini, and Clavdia puts matters more radically and more romantically when she teaches him that the essence of morality consists in exposing oneself to danger and sin, in "se perdre et même . . . se laisser dépérir." He who loses his life shall save it. This is not Castorp's final lesson; typically, he neither rejects nor completely accepts it, but it is a point of view with which he must come to terms, in that process of becoming free of the middle class which Mann once called the basic theme of all his works.

70

The mountain is not only the place of initiation; it is, as has often been observed, a microcosm of European society from 1907 to 1914. A recent commentator has objected that the novel "hoped to lay bare the conscience of a Europe teetering [*sic*] on the verge of a world war and . . . succeeded in describing the bourgeois conscience of a 'good' German . . ." This has the characteristic ring of the half-truth. Of course Mann sees Europe from a German point of view, more precisely, from the viewpoint of a German formed by Novalis and Wagner, Goethe and Nietzsche. But the consciences of Naphta and Settembrini, Clavdia and Peeperkorn are hardly "German bourgeois"; neither is Castorp's vision in the snow. Mann presents a pageant of Europe in a German perspective. Not every element of Europe is represented, but many of those omitted from the pageant, the French, let us say, or the aristocracy, or the proletariat, have their roles spoken by others.

Every significant inhabitant of the mountain is of course ill: not least the director of the sanatorium, the psychoanalyst, and the champion of reason and progress. It would be easier to dismiss this diagnosis as an example of German romantic morbidity if recent history had taken a different course. It is not the pessimism of the novel which seems dated or eccentric today; if anything, it is the hope, tentatively and cautiously expressed, that love may some time prevail over death.

Not the least of Mann's triumphs is his rendering of the almost irresistible attraction of the diseased world. It may be relevant to recall the medieval legend of a magnetic mountain, rising from the sea, which drew all ships to their destruction. On Mann's mountain, even the most robust succumb, or take to their heels in desperate flight, like Hans's Uncle James. As in *Buddenbrooks,* Mann suppresses no repulsive detail, and he revels in the comic and grotesque aspects of disease, but the effect of fascination is if anything increased. The book is not for the suggestible.

Castorp, "life's problem child," with his ambiguous gift for intellectual adventures and his aversion to the commercial struggle in Hamburg, is predestined for life "up there." Despite the warnings of Settembrini, the resolute champion of health, activity, and progress, and the example of his cousin Joachim, who lives only for the day when he can return to his duty, he succumbs without too much of a struggle. Mann recounts his enchantment in a leisurely and humorous manner, in the English fashion as he calls it, devoting almost a quarter of the long novel to the first three weeks. Time runs slowly when one's life is crowded with fresh experiences. Once Hans Castorp realizes his "disgraceful" love for Clavdia, he wills his illness and the "advantages of shame," willing at the same time the advantages of thought, dialectics, and the *vita contemplativa.* His initiation has begun in earnest.

In the first half of the novel, Castorp is characteristically "in the middle," caught between various persons all more "formed" and active than he. Settembrini and Ziemssen, the diseased champions of health, are opposed and outnumbered by the representatives of dissolution, the abnormal, the East, of "letting oneself go," the night, passion—all of these terms being roughly synonymous to Mann. The professional soldier Ziemssen may be "the best of all of the people up here"—Mann's tribute to the conservative values of the older Germany—but he is completely unintellectual and can do little to influence his cousin. More formidable is Ludovico Settembrini, the man of the Enlightenment, the apostle of liberal capitalism, bourgeois nationalism, and rationalism. His arguments are an amalgam of ideas and phrases taken from Petrarch, Voltaire, Schiller, Mazzini, the young Nietzsche, Heinrich Mann, and earlier works of Thomas Mann himself. It is not surprising that he often contradicts himself. A formidable and often brilliant talker, he is rhetorical rather than incisive, and his ideas, like his clothes, are threadbare. Hans's attitude towards Settembrini is ambivalent: the very decent humanist appears to him now as Satan, now as an organ-grinder, now as a well-meaning guardian. At bottom the humanist is afraid of all that is not clear and rational. This is his decisive weakness, and the day comes when his warnings are uttered in vain.

The psychoanalyst Krokowski is the least impressive champion of the forces of darkness. Settembrini's *mot:* "He has only one thought, and that's a dirty one," is tendentious, but one does not resent it, for the doctor, if not completely a charlatan, is of a clammy repulsiveness. His playing the role of Christ is one of the satiric pinnacles of the novel:

> Truly, he stood there, behind his little table, with arms outstretched and head bent to one side, and looked, despite his frock coat, like the Lord Jesus on the Cross.

> It turned out that Dr. Krokowski, at the end of his lecture, was making grand-style propaganda for the dissection of souls,

and with arms outspread summoned everyone to come unto him. Come unto me, he said, though in other words, ye who are weary and heavy-laden. And he left no doubt as to his conviction that all, without exception, were weary and heavy-laden.

Hans, almost pedantically determined to live dangerously, undergoes "analysis" at his hands. As is well known, Mann later vindicated Freud as an upholder of reason and light. His treatment of Krokowski does not necessarily indicate "resistance" to psychoanalysis as such; Freudians of Krokowski's type are not unknown.

Hofrat Behrens, the director of the sanatorium, is more subtly drawn. Doubtless he too is a bit of a charlatan. While one cannot accept Settembrini's denunciations at full value, Behrens has a certain aura of corruption: a Rhadamanthus with a financial interest in keeping Hades well filled. Yet there is no clear evidence against him; Behrens is one of those enigmatic borderline cases which particularly interest Mann. He is capable of unexpected human decency, but he is ill, driven by the intense eroticism of the mountain, unpredictable, and hence somewhat sinister. In Behrens' case, as elsewhere, Mann's irony approaches ambivalence. Peeperkorn, for instance, is both the "great personality" and an old fool; Castorp rises to a sublime vision but soon falls back into the old miasmal mist. Not that the net result of *The Magic Mountain* is zero, or anything approaching it, but it takes a sensitive and careful reader to solve its complicated equations.

Given his "primal experiences," Hans would in any case have been attracted to the "side" of the forbidden and the adventurous; his encounter with Clavdia Chauchat makes his course inevitable, all the more since the meeting has been prepared, so to speak, by his adolescent love for Pribislav Hippe. The two experiences are linked, both in reality and in Hans's dreams, by a classic Freudian symbol. Clavdia, languid, irresponsible, and always, so to speak, *en deshabille*, but with the charm Mann particularly associates with Russia, is perhaps the most brilliantly realized of all the persons of the novel. She is far from being crushed by the heavy weight of symbolical and mythological associations which she has to bear, but exists in her own right—unpredictable, exotic, sensuous— and of course diseased. She is by no means a mere brainless incarnation of the "eternal feminine" and one feels that Mann was less than gallant in naming her the "hot cat"; she has something of Lisaveta Ivanovna's flair for ideas. Yet essentially she is the temptress, white-armed, slant-eyed, with that reddish hair associated by Germanic tradition with sinister figures. As has been remarked, love appears in *The Magic Mountain* in its most primitive, naked form, and it drives Castorp for once beyond compromise and respectability. If one is dealing with Lilith or Venus, the conventions of the flatland do not apply and the gallantries of ordinary courtship appear absurd and insipid. During the first seven months of his passion, Hans barely speaks to Clavdia, finding instead a bizarre sublimation in the study of physiology, anatomy, and dermatology. It is Clavdia's body which has inspired these investigations, as his personification of life in her image (in the chapter "Research") makes clear enough. Hans's passions are "phlegmatic" but by no means weak, and that Clavdia is alien, forbidden, and, by his standards, evil is

75

of course an added stimulation. During his strangely retarded pursuit of Clavdia, his love has grown vaster than empires, if as slow. An almost unendurable tension is established.

The tension is resolved in the chapter "Walpurgis Night," one of the set pieces of the novel. After a rather light opening, an adroit parody of Goethe's "Walpurgisnacht" in *Faust*, Mann brings intellectual, psychological, and erotic strains together in a crashing climax. It is one of his most controlled, yet boldest performances, ranging from irony to a frenzy reminiscent of Stravinski's *Sacre du Printemps*. Settembrini is defeated by Clavdia: order and rationality, as such, will always be overthrown by passion. Hans learns from Clavdia the "Russian" lesson that true morality lies not with the virtuous, but with the great sinners. *Placet experiri!* Made bold by the freedom of the Mardi Gras and the use of a strange language—the German burgher instinctively slides into French in speaking to the *mondaine* temptress—Castorp launches into an impassioned hymn to the body, love, and death, which is at the same time a declaration of love and a rather exhaustive catalogue of Clavdia's person. It is Mann's most fevered treatment of a favorite theme. Hans, in his exalted and almost pathological state, does not shrink from the grotesque:

. . . Laisse-moi toucher dévotement de ma bouche l'Arteria femoralis qui bat au front de ta cuisse et qui se divise plus bas en les deux artères du tibia! Laisse-moi ressentir l'exhalation de tes pores et tâter ton duvet, image humaine d'eau et d'albumine, destinée pour l'anatomie du tombeau, et laisse-moi périr, mes lèvres aux tiennes!

Strange eloquence, compounded of physiology and libido, German thoroughness and German romanticism! Clavdia does not reject him; the appeal to the ethos of the *Liebestod* clinches matters, yet she leaves the sanatorium the next day, to come back only after an indefinite absence. The expectation of her return will hold Hans in the mountain world at least as surely as would her presence. As Settembrini remarks, he has tasted of the pomegranate. His fever curve, a reliable graph of the tensions of the novel, reaches a new peak.

After Clavdia's departure, *The Magic Mountain* becomes more abstract, more obviously the novel of ideas. Her place as the opponent of Western civilization is taken by Leo Naphta: the woman gives way to another man of words. Naphta is the dialectical antithesis to Settembrini; he is also an incarnated paradox: an anti-materialist Marxist, a Christian dedicated to hatred, a Jew turned Jesuit, an ascetic with a flair for luxury. He upholds the cult of blood, medievalism, terror, dictatorship, and war with arguments, largely drawn from the later Nietzsche, which often parallel Sorel's. Naphta is the John the Baptist of Fascism; one might say that Mann made him a Communist *faute de pire*. Mann takes him very seriously and for an obvious reason. In his radical repudiation of the whole liberal tradition, his championing of a non-rational *Kultur* against civilization, Naphta expresses, in exaggerated form, many of the ideas which Mann had himself developed in the *Reflections;* and it is significant that he almost invariably wins his countless dialectical battles with Settembrini. To the *Homo humanus* of the rationalist he opposes the concept of a fanatical and ascetic *Homo*

77

Dei. In acuity, logic, depth of learning, and intellectual courage, he far surpasses the champion of the West. Yet "his form is clarity, but his essence is confusion"; in a sense, Settembrini has the last word. As a human being, Naphta can be understood in terms of the trauma inflicted by hideous experiences in childhood. He not only represents death, he wills death: terror and sadism are essentially ends, not means. Killing is to him the "deepest joy," and his eventual suicide has the character of necessity.

Castorp, at first a passive spectator in the debates between East and West, comes gradually to play a respectable part of his own. He had already learned much from Settembrini, though he rarely came to conclusions of which his mentor approved; more from his hours of horizontal reading and reflection "checking up," as he called the latter, wrapped like a mummy in his deck-chair. At first, his increasing articulateness expresses itself largely in quotations picked up from his pedagogues, a way of speech which accords perfectly with Mann's technique of repeating a significant phrase. Often, by hurling a quoted tag into the argument, he achieves a remarkable effect. Eventually he begins to venture formulations and *aperçus* of his own. But until the brief epiphany in the snowstorm, he is unable to cope with either the liberal or the radical reactionary. He is "in the middle" in the bad sense, tossed back and forth in a sort of Zoroastrian conflict between light and darkness. And neither darkness nor light is to be trusted.

It is in the chapter "Snow" that Castorp at last frees himself from both his mentors and attains for a time a vision and a synthesis of his own. This is perhaps the most

magnificent passage in all Mann's work, and certainly the
high point of the novel. The style rises to new brilliance
and urgency, above all in the evocation of the snowstorm
with its "white darkness"—a formulation worthy of Milton—and of Castorp's dreams. Hans, somehow reinvig-
orated and conscious of a new dignity and a new inde-
pendence and eager to be alone with his reflections, sets
out into the mountains. Now his isolation is complete,
his education for the first time truly hermetic. He is
eager also for adventure and danger; his lonely journey
through the snowy landscape reminds him of the joy,
complicated and heightened by fear, of battling with
the breakers of the North Sea. He is dimly conscious of
willing to lose his way, just as he had lost it in the labyrin-
thine arguments of Settembrini and Naphta. Caught in a
sudden storm, half-frozen, Castorp falls asleep. Quite
literally, he is close to death; one may compare his condition to Joseph's in the pit, and recall Naphta's remarks
on the grave as a symbol of transmutation and magical
pedagogy. Hans's dream is a recapitulation and resolution of all that he has experienced on the mountain. He
dreams first of the "People of the Sun," serene, beautiful,
and statuesque; humane and consummately civilized.
They live on the shores of a southern sea, the "Sacred
Mediterranean" of Santayana. Obviously, the scene is
Greece—the classical Hellas of Winckelmann and Goethe,
the Apollonian Greece of Nietzsche. Yet the focus quickly
shifts: Castorp becomes aware of a Doric temple, enters
into it, and sees two hideous priestesses dismembering
and devouring a child. The world of high classicism exists
simultaneously with the cult of death; beneath civiliza-

tion lies *"Kultur,"* in Naphta's sense. The old antitheses! Yet Castorp, half-awakened, is able to reconcile them. The "People of the Sun" live with such exquisite humanity and form precisely because they know of cruelty and tragedy at the roots of life; they realize the power of death but do not abdicate before it; they create form because they are aware of the strength of dissolution. Settembrini, who acknowledges only the world of light, is a Philistine; but Naphta, who has betrayed that world, is evil. Both are wrong, and their endless playing-off of death against life, illness against health, spirit against nature, is essentially meaningless. Man must be "master of the antinomies": he must stand between them and understand life through his knowledge of death, and health through illness. Not Settembrini's reason, but love is stronger than death. Above all: *"For the sake of goodness and love, man shall not concede to death the mastery over his thoughts."*

This sentence marks the apex of Castorp's development and the great turning-point in Mann's career. It is clear that his condemnation of thinking in antitheses is self-criticism of the most incisive sort. His rejection of the cult of death marks a break with the German romantic tradition and hence with the dominant ideas of his own earlier career, from *Buddenbrooks* through the *Reflections.* "Death is a great power," but henceforth the supreme value is "friendliness to life"; all the more since life is the weaker force, which can maintain itself precariously at best. The implications are psychological and political as well as philosophic. The new humanism which Mann was later to uphold, with its belief that one must analyze and understand the non-rational for the sake of the rational, is a natural elaboration of the crucial doctrine of *The Magic Mountain*. His interpretation of Freud as the explorer of darkness for the sake of light, is another case in point. Indeed, the relation of the "Apollonian" world to the cannibalistic cult is an analogue of the relation of conscious to subconscious.

The "mediocre" Hans Castorp explains his vision by the remark that the world soul has dreamt through him. Mann later remarked that Castorp was only the apparent hero of *The Magic Mountain*: the real hero is Man; and clearly, Castorp plays the role of Everyman in the climactic section. But he is not the man to hold the experience firm in his grasp; after returning to the sanatorium, he no longer clearly understands it; he relapses, so to speak, from his representative role, though he continues to develop, on a rather modest scale, as an individual.

As Weigand has well shown, Castorp was also intended as a representative of the German, "bourgeois, humanist, and poet," and his education parallels the development of Germany from the romantic period to the First World War. This aspect of the work is perhaps the least convincing today, for Germany is understood in the novel as that problematic "other Germany," the land of poets and philosophers, the highly cultivated, moderate "land of the center." This was a concept defensible if already obsolescent when Mann wrote *The Magic Mountain*. Today it has only a melancholy historical interest, though one may hope that some day it will become relevant again. Mann has radically corrected his too optimistic idea of Germany in *Doctor Faustus*.

If *The Magic Mountain* had been only a novel of education, Mann might well have ended it with Castorp's dream. But it is of course a symbolic historical novel as well, and Castorp's development had to be traced down to 1914. Inevitably, everything that follows "Snow" is descending action; despite brilliant passages and sharp reversals, there is a relaxation of tension.

Just as Naphta is brought into the novel shortly after the first climactic scene of the "Walpurgis Night," Mynheer Pieter Peeperkorn is introduced soon after the greater climax of "Snow." He is the most bizarre of Mann's incarnated paradoxes. Although clearly a personality, he is, as Hans puts it, a "blurred personality." From the moment of his appearance in the sanatorium, he dominates the scene. His unending flow of remarks rarely makes logical sense—indeed, he is almost incapable of forming a complete sentence, yet he holds the center of the stage effortlessly; Settembrini and Naphta are completely overshadowed. Diseased, no longer young, he has the irresistible attraction of a nature-god. His half-articulate eloquence is devoted to the praise of the natural, non-rational forces of life, the "simple pleasures"—drink, food, and above all, of course, sex. As if to illustrate further the primacy of "life," he arrives in full possession of Clavdia, whom he encountered somewhere on his travels. Poor Hans has waited in vain: how can a bourgeois intellectual compete with the vital principle? At least he bears his displacement with dignity and tact.

Peeperkorn is a classic example of Mann's construction of a character synthetically, from a wide range of impressions and associations. As already noted, he is related to

82

Mann's conception of Tolstoi. Notoriously, he "is" also Gerhart Hauptmann in his personal appearance, his celebration of the passions, his intellectual insufficiency, and not least in his fabulous capacity for alcohol. It is thus no surprise to find him associated with Dionysus. But, startlingly, it becomes clear from Peeperkorn's repeated calls for bread and wine, the veiled references to the Trinity, and the parodistic supper at the sanatorium with his weary disciples, that he regards himself as a sort of Christ.

Castorp, like Clavdia, comes to feel that Peeperkorn is a majestic, truly regal figure. But his existence is threatened by a tragicomic paradox: this latter-day Dionysus, who regards the whole relation of man to life under the aspect of sexual intercourse, is obsessed by fears of impotence. When his virility fails, Peeperkorn commits suicide. The inadequacy of romantic vitalism *à la* D. H. Lawrence has never been more neatly demonstrated.

Hans's adjustment to the new situation is shown with great finesse. Fascinated by the "great personality," he soon overcomes his jealousy; so completely, in fact, that Clavdia is annoyed. Castorp after all finds the acquisition of new educational experiences more important than his own passions—an inhuman point of view, as Clavdia well notes. He cannot bear to address his beloved formally, yet does not dare to call her "Du" in the "kingly" presence of her new protector; precisely this awkward timidity makes Peeperkorn aware of his love. The consolidation of his strange friendship with Peeperkorn and of his new relation to Clavdia is handled with striking psychological skill. Peeperkorn's suicide precipitates a final reversal: Hans

83

and Clavdia speak of their love as "foolishness"—a rather degrading touch—and she leaves the mountain.

During his novitiate Castorp must be exposed to two further realms of experience: music and the occult. It is typical of him that his relation to music, while sincere, is a passive one: it is based on long hours of listening to the gramophone. His favorite records reflect the themes of his own experience: *Aïda* and *Carmen*, the struggle between honor and forbidden love; "L'après-midi d'un Faune," the escape from occidental activity to idyllic idleness; "Valentine's Farewell," from Gounod's *Faust*, the memory of the gallant Joachim, now dead after a brief return to service in the flatland; and finally, a single German piece, Schubert's "The Linden Tree"—representative of German romanticism and the "seductions of death," but also, by a curious dialectical twist to which we must return, of the overcoming of romanticism.

The "most questionable" of Castorp's adventures is his participation in a spiritualistic séance. In his *Experiences of the Occult* (1924), Mann makes it clear that he believes in the authenticity of certain mediums and their findings, though he finds the result of occult processes usually trivial, and the whole undertaking somehow unclean. Similarly, we are expected to take the sessions of the medium Elly Brand as repulsive—it is significant that the unappetizing Krokowski is in charge—but as literal fact. In the conjuring-up of Joachim, Mann breaks radically with all rationalistic realism: Ziemssen's "appearance" may be explained by mass suggestion, but he wears a German field helmet of the First World War, a type which was yet to be invented.

As the novel nears its end, its historical elements become more important and more obvious. "The Great Stupor" and later "The Great Irritation" brood over the mountain; after a period of boredom, bitter quarrels arise from the most trivial occasions. In this atmosphere, the charge of "infamy" which Settembrini hurls at Naphta leads inevitably to the duel which the well-meaning Hans tries, at the last moment, to prevent. The liberal's firing into the air is presumably no less symbolic than the totalitarian's suicide. The "thunderclap," the outbreak of war, is only the last of a series of explosions; the catastrophe brings a sense of relief. Finally the spell of the mountain is broken; Castorp, with crowds of others, rushes back to the flatland to play his part in the War. He would never have freed himself by his own energies, and shock has cured him after analysis failed.

Mann has been blamed for this resolution: Castorp's entrance into the battle can be read as a repudiation of the vision in the snow; death, dialectically defeated, is historically victorious. On some levels, such criticism is absurd: given Castorp's background and character, to say nothing of his role as the representative German burgher, what else could he be expected to do? He is no political radical, still less a pacifist. Yet one may wish, perhaps, that Mann had regarded the coming of the War more critically. Life, we read, has accepted its problem child after his sojourn in the mountain of sin. Undoubtedly, this reflects Mann's own experience of 1914, and there is no point in caviling. But one may recall that while Castorp was hastening from the Swiss mountains to the warring flatlands, Hermann Hesse and Romain Rolland, less am-

85

biguous friends of life, were traveling in the opposite direction. There remains an inexpugnable contrast between conservative dialectics and consistent directness. Mann can leave us only the hope that out of death, love may some day arise.

To say that it is Castorp's fate to fight in a war whose causes he does not understand would be to tell less than the whole truth. Presumably, he is defending the "land of the center" against the extremes of East and West. We see him for the last time on a Belgian battlefield, singing a song symbolic of death and romanticism. But we have been told that the man who dies for the "magic song" actually is dying not for it but for the conquest of romanticism, for love, for the future. The argument is as complicated as it is, to the non-dialectical mind, unconvincing.

Perhaps the resolution of the novel has already suggested what seems to be the actual case: that *The Magic Mountain* is a brilliant work of literature, not an infallible nor always a profound work of philosophy. Still less of politics! Some of the philosophical constructions are magnificent; others not. There is a certain intoxication with thinking in antitheses, and a supersaturation with the ideas of Nietzsche (whom Mann vastly overrated at this period) and of the earlier German romanticists, Novalis above all.

Some of the most amusing moments of the novel—the malapropisms of Frau Stöhr, for instance, or the "good" and "bad" Russian tables—are likely to be neglected by the critic because they call for no interpretation. One is apt also to be unconscious, in the easy flow of the narrative, of the scope of Mann's style, which ranges from the realism of the account of Joachim's death to the visionary; from the grotesque to the gently or mordantly ironic. The pace is equally varied. It is hardly necessary to add that the whole work is held together by an enormous net of leitmotifs, used more subtly than in *Buddenbrooks,* though without quite the musicality of *Tonio Kröger.* Mann once accused himself of a tendency to lose sight of measure and proportion in his writing, and few readers have found *The Magic Mountain* unduly brief; but there is a grand, architectural symmetry: the action rises to its first peak in the night of the Mardi Gras, descends, rises again to Castorp's dream, and then falls gradually to the ending.

Whatever its ambiguities, *The Magic Mountain* stands as the supreme German novel of ideas. In Mann's development it marks a turn away from an exclusive preoccupation with the artist towards an interest in man, a shift from the special case to the typical and universal.

Disorder and Early Sorrow (1925) is one of Mann's less ambitious pieces, yet within its limits one of his most successful. With its lightness, its understatement, its location in the private world of Mann's Munich home, it seems to lie at a far remove from *The Magic Mountain.* Yet it is linked with that novel in various ways, most notably by an ironic "friendliness to life." Its hero, in a sense, is German middle-class culture, a "problem child" threatened by the inflation of the Twenties and by the "Bolshevistic" ideas current in Germany in that decade. Yet, as in *Buddenbrooks,* the ideological element is kept tactfully in the background.

Mann writes here with the deftness and precision, but none of the bitterness, of the best of his early short stories. The evidence of disorder is everywhere: in the boy Snapper's "labile and irritable nervous system" no less than in Professor Cornelius' "8000-mark beer" or the "two formerly bourgeois sisters" who have sunk to the servant class. But there are no Wagnerian gestures or big words; even the death theme (Cornelius, as a historian, loves what is past, fixed, and eternal) is handled briefly and with a certain grace. An enlightened conservative, the Professor accepts the new universe with a sort of wry affection. The relations within the family, with its contrapuntally arranged pairs of children, Ingrid and Bert, Snapper and Elly, are treated with an unsentimental tenderness.

The "disorder" of the milieu parallels of course the tumult within the psyche of the five-year-old Elly, who falls violently "in love" with a well-meaning and quite commonplace student who has danced with her as a joke. Elly is adored by her father this side idolatry: the psychological implications are clear, but the danger of becoming stickily Freudian and problematic is neatly avoided. Nietzsche once remarked that it is the fate of the Germans to "get heavy about everything." In *Disorder and Early Sorrow*, Mann has escaped the general fate of his countrymen.

Even the earlier sketch *A Man and His Dog* (1918), another directly autobiographical account of life in Munich, shares the new humaneness and relatively cheerful irony. Experts in canine psychology have maintained that the dog Bashan is admirably drawn. However this may be, he too bears witness to Mann's new orientation. For

Bashan, unlike the ultrarefined Percy of *Royal Highness*, is no decadent, marked dog. While once "nervous and anemic," he has now adjusted himself to life. Mann analyzes his physique and character elaborately, with a sort of affectionate naturalism and much humor. The pace may seem excessively deliberate to persons not particularly devoted to dogs.

One can describe the change in Mann's intellectual standpoint since the First World War by saying that he has moved further and further from Naphta's position without becoming Settembrini. A keen and sometimes tragic awareness of "the depths which lie below" distinguishes his "Third Humanism," as he has called it, from optimistic rationalism.

To a large extent his development seems to have been determined by political factors. The salutary shock of the German defeat of 1918; the friendly reception he received on trips abroad after the War, which broke down his sense of isolation and made him aware of a certain solidarity among European intellectuals; and the feeling of repugnance at the rise of Fascism and Nazism must all have had their effect. In Munich, where Mann had long made his home, the danger of Hitlerism was more evident than elsewhere in Germany; it was the favorite city of political adventurers as well as of the German *bohème*. His *The German Republic* (1922) is evidence of a heightened sense of social responsibility. No longer "non-political," Mann felt called upon not only to represent Germany to Europe but to assume, in domestic affairs, the role of *praeceptor Germaniae*. Particularly after the award of the Nobel Prize in 1929, it seemed an appropriate part, and he played it with distinction and intellectual courage, if not with practical success. The essays on Lessing and on "Freud's Position in the History of Modern Thought" and the eloquent "Appeal to Reason" best illustrate Mann's increasing concern with politics. In *Mario and the Magician* (1929), he gave high aesthetic form to a treatment of political matters—a feat which in his earlier days he would have declared impossible.

Not that *Mario* is a bald political allegory. Mann once remarked that it is "a tale with moral and political implications"; it has also, besides its value as a story on the literal level, implications about the relation of the "daemonic" artist to his public. Mann may well have remembered that Nietzsche had called Wagner "the old magician."

Yet quite clearly the political element is of central importance. From any other point of view the novella seems to lack unity, falling into two disparate parts: the apparently trivial events in the Grand Hotel and on the beach, and the terrifying account of the performance given by the magician Cipolla. Once one sees Fascism in the crowds at the resort and the Fascist leader in Cipolla, the structure becomes clear; the seemingly formless takes shape. The first part, serving as a prelude, gives an added force to the second; and of course, the converse is true also: one can best understand the "patriotic" children, the Italian in the bowler hat, and so on, retrospectively, after getting to know the magician and his victims. The incidents of the plot, which seem but loosely strung together, are actually combined into a unity of the most

90

careful design; and one should not be deceived by the casual, anecdotal style.

Within the two main divisions of the story, the structure is developed symmetrically. In the first part, events rise in significance from the slight and seemingly irrelevant annoyances of the Grand Hotel to the incident of the naked child on the beach. This is a semi-comic crisis, but still a crisis: the first head-on clash with the Fascist mind. After a sort of philosophical intermezzo, the scene changes to Cipolla's performance. The same process of intensification is repeated, though this time on a more serious—and more obviously political—level. The focus has shifted from a group more or less tainted with Fascism to a leader who gradually bends the crowd to his will. The magician's feats advance from the comic and apparently harmless through the grotesque to the horrible. Gradually a situation is built up which can be resolved only tragically. Fascism is seen throughout from the point of view of the highly cultivated patrician, and equated with the lower middle-class vulgarity of the crowd at the seashore. Without denying the attractive qualities of the Italians, Mann implies—of course for the benefit of his German audience—that Italy is a politically backward nation which could never serve as a model for the more enlightened *Reich*.

It is in the appearance and character of Cipolla that the political implications of the novella are most clearly brought out. Again and again he has recourse to two great sources of power in carrying out his "magic": the claw-handled whip and the stimulus of cognac. Force and fraud, as it were; and Mann draws our attention to these symbols with almost Wagnerian insistence. Cipolla is a mixture of apparently contradictory traits; he looks like a "charlatan and mountebank," a veritable Cagliostro; yet like the *petite bourgeoisie* on the beach he is completely devoid of humor. There is something almost fantastically old-fashioned about his dress. (In the essays and speeches in which Mann warned the Germans of the implications of Fascism, it was precisely its reactionary, "old-fashioned" character which he stressed.) Cipolla combines boastfulness and self-pity; he claims that it is he who suffers, not his victims, during his feats of hypnotism. He paints himself, in other words, as the all-wise, all-enduring hero, the leader of the people; or as the romantic artist who "suffers" for mankind. His arrogance is an obvious compensation for ugliness and deformity; his sensitiveness about "national honor" repeats that of the bowler-hatted man on the beach. Above all: one must not underrate the magician's powers; he gradually reveals himself as "the most powerful hypnotist I have ever seen in my life." (One remembers that he had billed himself as a mere prestidigitator.) As artist—and he is not primarily the artist—Cipolla differs radically from Mann's earlier representations of the type. He has none of that frustrated and ironic love for ordinary humanity which distinguished Tonio Kröger and all the others.

By flattery, tricks, intimidation, and above all by hypnotic powers, Cipolla subdues almost the entire audience. Even the aristocrats, including an army officer, a lady of cultural pretensions, and a "long-toothed Anglo-Saxoness" fall under his spell. The spectators, it is worth noting, have never liked the magician, and generally show sympathy for his victims. Yet no one leaves the performance; Cipolla exudes fascination as a person, "independently of the program." A new theme is introduced: this is a story of the will, as well as of Fascism, and the elements of moral and political tyranny are closely interrelated and finally fused into one.

A certain gentleman from Rome, who has made the most stubborn and courageous effort to resist, finally submits to Cipolla's will and finds that he is happier after yielding. The Roman, who is sympathetically presented, has no positive goal; this "fighter for freedom," as Mann calls him with a certain irony, is therefore doomed. As Nietzsche observed, one must be free to some end; merely to be free from something is not of particular significance. Like Settembrini, the Roman does not understand the "forces stronger than reason or virtue" to which the merely rational must always succumb.

How then can the magician be overthrown? Mario, who finally strikes him down, is a person of no particular distinction; quite the contrary. Despite the heroic and republican associations of his name he can hardly be taken as the champion of militant democracy or free will, but his action has symbolic significance. Mario is notable only because he is unusually likable and decent. He has been trained to obey; he has no desire for a clash with Cipolla and tries to escape from him before the crisis occurs. Mario strikes only when the magician, in his *hubris*, humiliates him beyond endurance; he acts from some instinctive sense of personal dignity. This dignity, Mann seems to imply, is in itself a force stronger than free will or the conscious mind; it brings down the tyrant after

93

they have failed. Cipolla lies on the platform, "a huddled heap of clothing"; and one cannot help thinking of the corpse of Mussolini exposed in the square at Milan. There is an end of terror; the tragedy is finished. One is left with the sense of liberation, a liberation both political and human.

6. MYTH AND PSYCHOLOGY

IN HIS "SUFFERING AND GREATNESS OF RICHARD WAGNER,"
Mann wrote, in 1933, of the nineteenth century's love of
the "monumental and grandiosely massive, combined, remarkably enough, with an infatuation for the minutely
small, the psychological detail." Later in the same essay,
he speaks of "naturalism which rises to the symbolic and
grows to the mythic"; still later, of Wagner's tendency to
"the backward view, self-quotation, and dissolution." The
essay appeared in the same year as the first volume of
Joseph and His Brothers (1933–43), and it is clear that
Mann used it to characterize his own intention as well as
Wagner's. *Joseph* then, with its shift from realism to
symbolism, from the present to the mythical past, from
a concern with decadence to an increasingly optimistic
affirmation of belief in the future, seems at first glance to
be radically different from anything that Mann had attempted before.

Yet of course there are lines of development connecting

Joseph with Mann's earlier work. From one point of view it appears as a completion, one might almost say a correction, of *The Magic Mountain.* If the ending of the earlier novel blurred, to some extent, its intention, there is no similar ambiguity here. The basic tenet of "friendliness to life," precariously attained by Castorp, is now accepted as axiomatic. The cult of death has lost its magnetic attraction, and has become, in its manifestation in Egyptian religion, an obsolete and often comic affair. One notes also that Mann's preoccupation, in *Joseph,* with universal characters, has its precedents: Settembrini and Naphta, for example, are symbolic archetypes too. Even the "mythic thinking" of the tetralogy, with its daring identifications and combinations, was foreshadowed in earlier works; for surely Mann's own habitual mode of thought, tending to loose associations and strained antitheses, betrayed an affinity to the mythical long before he ventured the descent into the deep well of the past. The novelty of *Joseph* is a matter of emphasis and degree.

The vast project, which was to occupy Mann, with interruptions, for some sixteen years, had various roots. He tells of a boyhood enthusiasm for Egyptian culture; of a request, made about 1926, that he write an introduction to a series of pictures illustrating the story of Joseph; of reading Goethe's remark that its treatment in the Bible was "most charming . . . only it seems too short, and one feels oneself called to work it out in detail." Mann remarks also that it is natural for the mature writer to turn to the typical and mythical. Perhaps more decisive was the German intellectual climate of the 1920's, with its tendency to glorify the non-rational and the subconscious, to give the concept of the myth a strongly anti-intellectual and often reactionary character. The revival, for example, of Bachofen's cult of the "primeval motherly," or Ludwig Klages' attack on the intellect, or Alfred Bäumler's interpretation of Nietzsche's philosophy as a *mythos* of brutality, are cases in point. Obviously, Mann was as sensitive as anyone to the fascination of "the darkness of the past and the night of the unconscious" but far more aware than most of where the fashionable worship of instinct could lead. He decided on a characteristic manoeuvre: to combine the mythical element with a highly rational, sophisticated psychology, to treat a "dark," primitive subject under the aspect of reason and light. Just as Castorp had taken over the concept of the *Homo Dei* from the obscurantist Naphta and filled it with a humane content, Mann resolved to wrest the myth from the reactionaries and parlor Fascists. Thus Mann's turn to the past was not primarily an attempt to "escape," though doubtless his immersion in the Hebrew and Egyptian worlds served to some extent as a refuge from the threatening present.

Like *The Magic Mountain, Joseph* was first planned as a novella. This time Mann was even more strikingly deceived about the scope of his undertaking; the complete work has over 2100 pages. In part, his characteristic thoroughness was responsible for this fantastic expansion. He found it necessary to devote a whole volume to Joseph's ancestors, and Jacob almost became the dominant figure of the tetralogy. Not content with Genesis as a source, Mann consulted various other books of the Bible, Hebrew commentaries such as the *Midrash, Sepher Hay-*

ashar, and *Rashi;* the Koran; and Persian poets like Jāmī and Firdusī. Treatments of the story of Joseph are almost numberless, and Mann seems to have devoted a vast amount of study to them alone. In addition there were works of Egyptology, Orientology, comparative mythology and religion; and a great deal of Freudian and Jungian psychology. The abundance of polymathic learning recalls Joyce, and leads, in *Joseph,* to a rather overwhelming increase of the encyclopedic strain already evident in *The Magic Mountain.* The older Mann has a certain inclination to excessive bulk; in the tetralogy, this tendency seems to have been strengthened by the example of three works: Wagner's *Ring,* the second part of *Faust* with its playful and very extended treatment of mythology, and the ultradigressive *Tristram Shandy.*

Despite the wealth of scholarship which Mann exploited in writing *Joseph,* the work is not, in any important sense, a historical novel. Its intention is less to recreate a period of the past than to show typical and timeless figures against a more or less distinct background. Even when the treatment of the milieu approaches, in sharp detail, the "realism" of the conventional historical novel, its symbolic aim is still primary. Accordingly, instead of trying to avoid anachronisms, Mann finds an ironic pleasure in weaving them into the fabric of the story. In emulation of *Faust,* Mann has attempted here to create universal human characters. He intends in other words not to recapture the past as such but to reveal basic human archetypes as they recur in the myths of the gods, in legend, and in history. *Joseph* can best be considered as a philosophical and frankly didactic prose epic, nearly as remote from any conventional genre as is, say, *Ulysses*. Mann, who has himself remarked that "it almost looks as though nothing counts any more in the domain of the novel except what is no longer a novel," has little interest in further achievement within the traditional forms.

For dealing with universals—no easy task in fiction—the narrative method of repetition and variation which Mann had cultivated throughout his career was an appropriate instrument. His method, essentially, was to expand his old technique of the leitmotif; in *Joseph*, it is not merely phrases which are repeated: actions, situations, and characters return again and again. Thus the enmity between Joseph and his brethren was prefigured by the hostility between Jacob and Esau, Isaac and Ishmael, Cain and Abel; and, on the divine plane, by the strife between Osiris and Set. The fundamental patterns are not limited to the human level: Mann uses the Babylonian notion of a revolving sphere, according to which a given action will be played out now among gods, now among men. A variety of mythologies, Hebrew, Christian, Greek, Syro-Phoenician, Egyptian, and Babylonian, are drawn upon and interrelated. Associations and identities between the various gods appear, the myths seem to grow together, and gradually the concept of a genuine monotheism grows out of this rife multiplicity. Joseph himself, who must go down into the pit, die, and be born again, is associated with the grain which perishes to be reborn, and thus with a whole series of divine figures: Osiris, Adonis-Tammuz, Dionysus Zagreus, and, by anticipation, Jesus Christ. Numerous other examples could be given. In fact, the whole mass of characters and events in *Joseph* can be reduced by association to a few basic ideas and types. That which returns repeatedly, then, is the mythic, and is precisely the universal at which Mann aims.

In this mode of experiencing the world, Mann is indebted to Nietzsche's concept of eternal recurrence, to Goethe's idea of primal types, and to Jung's archetypes. His first problem, obviously, was to make "mythical living" credible; an entirely different psychology was required. The "Prelude" and much of the rest of the first volume, *The Tales of Jacob*, are devoted to reorienting the reader in time and to introducing him to a prelogical way of thought. The past, we are told, is a deep and bottomless well: we cannot descend into it without a shudder. Yet though the mystery of the beginnings of things is unsolvable, there is no need to despair, for we are to journey downwards "only" three thousand years. Jacob and his contemporaries were not really very different from us—the historical imagination need not be too greatly strained—but they are marked by a certain "dreamy inexactitude" in their thinking. More precisely, their sense of individuality was ambiguous: a man of the patriarchal age might say "I" in speaking of a deed done by his mythic prototype and namesake hundreds of years before. The case of Eliezer, Jacob's chief servant, is the neatest example. There seems to have been "an" Eliezer, always the chief servant of the tribal patriarch, since the days of Abraham; and again, two historical Abrahams, far separated in time, have coalesced in the myth. As Mann notes, it is difficult to tell the stories of "people who do not quite know who they are," who identify themselves more or less completely with their predecessors. This way of thought is "moon grammar," characteristic of moods of exaltation, and on occasion it may extend to tense as well as to person. While ordinary people say "it was," the mythically enlightened think in terms of an eternal present. Though the uninitiated believe, for example, that Adonis-Tammuz dies and is resurrected every year, the wise know that these actions of the god, like all fundamental events of religion and of life itself, exist outside of time. It is the celebration of a rite which best frees one from the illusion of time, and the festival is thus one of the major themes of the novel. In a way, Mann notes, the practitioners of moon grammar "knew who they were" more clearly than does modern man; for the sense of "living a myth" gives the individual the pleasure of recognition and a feeling of continuity and stability which legitimizes his existence. The point anticipates Mr. Joseph Campbell's fervid exhortation, in *The Hero with a Thousand Faces,* to cure ourselves of civilization's discontents by living mythically.

Essentially, the "Prelude" is musical in function. In its first sentence, the image of the well is introduced, which is to become in its variations of pit and grave the symbol of the past, the subconscious, death, and the womb, and thus is one of the most important leitmotifs of the novel. Further themes and images, among others the moon, the festival, the angels and their jealousy, are gracefully woven in. The tone ranges from solemnity to benevolent irony; the style from the lyrical to the overexplicit. In a very Mannian myth which deals with the erotic interrelations of spirit, soul, and body, the idea of the synthesis, the blessing from heaven above and the depths below, is introduced.

Dominated though it is by the idea of recurrence, the world of the tetralogy still has a place for change. On the religious and mythical level, the notion of substitution is decisive: Esau, though he "is" Cain, does not kill his brother. For God Himself is changing and developing; an action which He would have regarded with favor in one generation may evoke His wrath in a later one. On the human plane as well as the divine, the changes, the variations of the motifs, are in the direction of the good. Mann does not lapse into a belief in uncomplicated, unilinear progress—he reminds us that "progress" may lead to overrefinement, decadence, and even to loss of the blessing—but the general direction of the work is a forward one.

This Goethean optimism of the novel is also evident in the development of its hero, for Joseph, like Faust, rises through repeated metamorphoses to the fullest realization of his personality. *Joseph,* among other things, is a *Bildungsroman,* on an even more inclusive scale than *The Magic Mountain,* for in the Biblical novel, the whole tribe of Abraham, and its God, are undergoing a cosmic process of education. More clearly than in *The Magic Mountain,* man himself is the hero; "the birth of the Ego out of the mythical collective," as Mann puts it, is one of the central themes. As the Ego approaches maturity, the myth is increasingly humanized; the world becomes more rational and "modern."

Joseph, at the beginning of the story, is a *Wunderkind,*

102

attractive, self-conscious, and aggravating as only a youthful prodigy can be. He is so beautiful that people often take him for a god, and as brilliant in rational calculation as in the subtleties of "moon grammar." While he can enter without difficulty into the mythical universe of his father, he is more modern, more sophisticated and worldly, than Jacob. As a transitional figure, he is endangered; and his position is made doubly precarious by his "eagerness for new things," his joy in forbidden thoughts. He too is a "problem child of life," though far more gifted than Hans Castorp; he too, in his delight in playing with ideas, even with the idea that he is a "little god," is an analogue of the artist. The first chapter of the novel, showing Joseph sitting half-naked by a well, playing at the worship of the moon, and adroitly parrying the rebukes of his doting father, suggests his flair for adventure, his fabulous charm, and the slyness which later lets him assume the role of the roguish Hermes. Contemplating the moon, Joseph falls into a half-trance, the sign of a spiritual endowment which is a danger as well as a blessing. Later, when he has become the enormously successful man of affairs, the ecstatic side of his nature is largely lost.

If Joseph is problematic, it is of course Jacob who has made him so. The first volume puts the father's adoration into perspective: it is largely the story of Jacob and Rachel, of the seven years of waiting, the long-frustrated hope for a son, and Rachel's bitter sufferings at Joseph's birth. Jacob loves her in a way which stirs the jealousy of his God; and when he speaks of Joseph, in mythical terms, as the "son of a virgin," or, borrowing a phrase from the cult of Adonis, as "the true son," he seems wilfully to invite God's wrath as well as Leah's. After Rachel dies in giving birth to Benjamin, her second son, Jacob concentrates his idolatrous love on Joseph, who has inherited her beauty and the "night of her eyes." Joseph's conviction that "other people love him more than they do themselves" is an understandable error.

With its psychological tensions and sudden reversals, the story of Jacob, Rachel, and Leah is the most vivid in all the tetralogy, and in Jacob's love for his "true wife" and "true son" lies most of the tenderness and human warmth of the novel. Despite its disquisitions on "moon grammar" and the all-too-learned sections of the "Prelude," *The Tales of Jacob* is the least bookish and Alexandrian of the four volumes. Mann has repeatedly represented paternal love with feeling and charm, in works ranging from *Disorder and Early Sorrow* to *Doctor Faustus,* but never more effectively than here. In the relation of Jacob and Rachel he has shown, for the first time, a "real" marriage, without sentimentality but without understatement.

Joseph's great opinion of his own gifts, all the more annoying because it is well founded, is evident enough in the Biblical account of his two dreams. Mann has added a third, still more flagrantly egotistical; his Joseph is clearly predestined to the pit. A mysterious and sardonic messenger, who guides Joseph to his infuriated brethren, serves to remind the reader that everything is taking place in accordance with God's plan. (The messenger, who had already appeared, in a different shape, to Jacob, is an amalgam of a jealous Hebrew angel, the Egyptian Anubis, and Hermes Psychopompos; later, he escorts Jo-

seph to Egypt.) The brothers play the role of Cain to
Joseph's Abel. But they must "live the myth" in a relatively
humane way: instead of killing him they tear to pieces
his coat of many colors, neatly identified by Mann with
the veil which Rachel had worn.

In his descent into the pit, Joseph takes some comfort
in associating himself with the slain Adonis, the original
"true son" who rose again after three days in the earth.
Yet he is frightened and chastened; never again will he
be the *enfant terrible*. But he realizes that he must have
willed the catastrophe—among his gifts is a preternatural,
indeed Freudian sharpness of insight into his own subconscious—and after he has been resurrected, he makes
no attempt to return to his father's home. Jacob, by ar-
rogating to himself in his treatment of his sons the par-
tiality reserved to Jehovah, has also willed disaster.

The Midianite merchant who draws Joseph from the
"womb" is the first of a series of substitute fathers who
watch over his fortunes. All of them—the merchant, Potiphar's steward Mont-kaw, Potiphar himself, and Mai-
Sachme, the governor of the Egyptian prison which serves
as another of Joseph's pits—single him out for particular
favors. But Joseph, though filled with a sense of a sure
if mysterious destiny, always behaves with tact.

With his practical talents and his charismatic aura,
Joseph makes a brisk beginning in his new career. That
he is in fact a slave is of little importance: people associate him, willy-nilly, with some divine prototype, with
Thot, the god of scribes, with Thot's Greek analogue
Hermes, and most significantly with Osiris, to whose role
he cunningly adapts himself. Osiris is the Egyptian

equivalent of Adonis-Tammuz; his part comes to Joseph very naturally. He has changed his name to Osarsiph (that is, "The Osiris Joseph," "The Dead Joseph"); it also recalls the legend of the infant Osiris among the reeds. Thus the Egyptians tend to believe that he "is" a divine foundling, just as he had intended. In going to Egypt Joseph is descending into another pit, for the "nether kingdom" is the land of worship of the past, rigid conservatism, unabashed phallicism, and, to the Hebrews, the realm of the dead. Joseph regards his new environment with a mixture of excited curiosity and religious disdain. "Its dead are gods and its gods—what are they?" To his father, Egypt was an abomination; Joseph has the more complicated attitude of a later generation.

Joseph's life in Egypt is recounted in a way which contrasts rather sharply with the tone of the volumes devoted to patriarchal life. *Joseph in Egypt* (1936) is centered on the passion of Potiphar's wife, and thus partakes of the tensions and attractions of the "normal" erotic novel. Mann has also made use of more abundant concrete data in dealing with the Egyptian scene; his elaborate descriptions of cities and costumes, his accounts of Egyptian economics, politics, and religion, give a degree of documentation which approaches at times that of the conventional historical novel. The atmosphere is less mythic, more rational. In addition, a picaresque strain is often evident. Joseph, as we know, is associated with the roguish Hermes, and many of the chapter headings have an arch ring reminiscent of Sterne. Accordingly, the style is at times idiomatic and relatively light; but at others, it is so ponderous that one sympathetic and highly qualified critic has suspected deliberate self-parody.

Joseph's first experiences in Egypt are not dissimilar to his father's during his earlier sojourn in Mesopotamia, another "underworld." The essential difference is that the Egyptian sphere is more perilous, and Joseph himself is more complicated and problematic than Jacob. But Joseph's success clearly repeats his father's economic victories over Laban, recounted in *The Tales of Jacob*. He is indeed almost too successfully a virtuoso in flattery, but essentially, for all his shrewdness, a man of good will. It is this unexpected integrity which finally disarms the suspicions of the steward Mont-kaw, and leads to Joseph's elevation in Potiphar's house.

"Osarsiph" must walk carefully on his new path, for Potiphar's household, like Egypt itself, is the scene of a fundamental religious and political conflict. The old order of rigid conservatism and exclusive nationalism has its representatives there, who are shocked by the rise of the "wretched" outlander. On the other side are arranged the liberals—cosmopolitan, tolerant, eager for foreign innovations. To this party Potiphar himself belongs; his wife Mut to the reactionary group. The "good" dwarf, Schepses-Bes, Joseph's friend, is opposed by the chauvinistic Dûdu; the pygmies play the roles of comical good and bad angels.

More fundamental than the political and religious threat to Joseph is the erotic, though the strands are almost inextricably interwoven. It comes as no surprise to readers of Mann that the realm of death is the realm of sex; that Mut, the temptress, is a worshiper of the dead

107

past; or that the reactionary Dûdu furthers her plans for reasons of his own. Mann has mustered all his psychological talents to reinterpret the story; it is perhaps the most extreme example of his Freudianization of the myth. Others before him have read Genesis 39:1 to mean that Potiphar was a eunuch (most scholars hold that the Hebrew word denotes merely "courtier" here). Mann derives this defect from the turbulent state of Egyptian religion: Potiphar's bewildered parents had caused his emasculation in a well-meaning attempt to appease the new religious forces. Their incestuous marriage, while of course in the older Egyptian tradition, had come to seem sinister; they had made the sacrifice out of *Angst*. Others before Mann had undertaken to vindicate Potiphar's wife—some writers even inventing a happy ending —but none can have devoted more care and ingenuity to her rehabilitation.

Mann's heroine was not born for the role of seductress; she appears first as a "moon nun," a priestess of Amun-Re, cool, elegant, and rather snobbish. She is overcome by a revolution of the subconscious, not without a struggle. Yet when she asks Potiphar to have Joseph removed from the household, she phrases the request so tactlessly that it is clear that she really intends to be refused. The "conscience of the flesh" has triumphed over the honor of the mind. Her frenzy increases through three years of frustration, until she is ready to kill her husband; or, assuming the part of the ambivalent goddess Ishtar, to slay her reluctant lover.

Mann traces Mut's passion in detail, with perhaps more thoroughness than verve. Somewhat older than Joseph, she has feelings for him which are in part maternal (the classic Freudian mixture); her name in fact means "mother." She dreams of cutting herself severely and of hoping that Joseph will "still her blood." This motif is repeated in the delicious chapter "The Ladies' Party," in which all of Mut's female friends are so distracted by Joseph's beauty that they "accidentally" cut themselves with fruit knives. Yet Mut's conscious mind puts up a gallant fight: in the effort to keep from uttering the notorious invitation to Joseph, she bites her tongue so severely that the words finally emerge as "Thleep with me!" (It is typical of *Joseph in Egypt* that this ironic naturalistic touch robs the scene of most of its emotional charge.) Mut's degradation is complete when she turns to the grotesque African hag Tabubu for love charms; during the obscene ritual she herself appears almost as a witch. After the decisive rejection by the alien Joseph she reverts to the exclusive nationalism of her party—a particularly nice touch—even calling her slaves "Egyptian brothers" in inciting them to punish the Hebrew upstart.

For he indeed has not completely outgrown his earlier *hubris,* as his allusion to himself as the "son of a virgin" indicates. More precisely, his old instinct to play expresses itself in the protracted flirtation with Mut—the artist side gets the better of the burgher, so to speak. He plays with his own freedom of action, evading a clear decision, invents sophistic reasons for not avoiding Mut, and disregards the warnings of the good Bes, that miniature Settembrini. Joseph has seven reasons for preserving his chastity (another touch of self-parody?), which resolve themselves into one: that at the critical moment he sees "the countenance of the father." One must take "father" in the broadest sense: the face is Jacob's of course, but it is also the face of other fathers, Mont-kaw, Potiphar, and above all of God. It reminds Joseph that he is a Hebrew; in other words, of the danger of sin, a concept for which the Egyptians do not even have a word. So Joseph does not "fall," though he has passed the test by the barest of margins. That there is something a bit comic about masculine chastity Mann would seem to realize as well as Fielding did. His hero can cut no glorious figure, pass or fail—another indication of the picaresque quality of *Joseph in Egypt*.

A relaxed, not too serious tone is also evident in the account of Joseph's punishment. The admirable Potiphar, having sensed that Joseph was the pursued rather than the pursuer, judged his beloved "son" more leniently than the would-be pander Dûdu; but Joseph, at the very least, has violated the commandments of decorum and must be removed to restore the situation. In his pallid way, Potiphar is one of the most attractive figures of the tetralogy. His existence is a bitterly empty and representative one, devoted to sheer form, and one recalls that Tonio Kröger used "eunuch" as one of his symbols of the artist. But Potiphar plays his part with dignity and courage.

The last volume of the tetralogy, *Joseph the Provider* (1943), also has picaresque touches, but its atmosphere approaches that of a very sophisticated fairy tale, a "didactic fairy tale" like *Royal Highness*. The epic becomes increasingly ironic as it approaches its end; the characters repeatedly remind each other that they are "in a story"; and Mann teases the reader with deliberate retardations

and long asides. Yet the recognition scene and the be-
stowal of the blessing—the climaxes of the outer and inner
actions respectively—have genuine power.

Joseph's stay in the Egyptian prison, a pit where he
must remain for three years, is not disagreeable; his sojourn with the amiable warden Mai-Sachme must be one
of the most *gemütlich* imprisonments in literature. It becomes so obvious that God's favor is with him that his
success appears increasingly inevitable, and Mann treats
the data of the legend more and more lightly. Joseph's
interpretation of the dreams of the court officials and his
release from prison are set in the comic mode. Even when
he "stands before Pharaoh," summoned in a matter of no
slight importance, the tone is not greatly changed: Joseph "is" Hermes, the god of brilliant rogues and sharp
businessmen, though he is to serve Pharaoh loyally and
well. Even among Mann's characters, Joseph appears complex: a devoted administrator and a bit of a scamp, godly
and worldly, a Hebrew who has almost become an Egyptian.

Mann's Pharaoh is a gifted decadent, or better a diseased
genius, of the kind he has always found fascinating. His
first knowledge of the historical Amenhotep IV (who later
called himself Ikhnaton or Akhenaten) must have given
Mann a thrill of recognition, for the Egyptian seems actually to have belonged to the type of his earlier heroes; it is
not surprising that he decided to incorporate Ikhnaton
into the legend of Joseph. Pharaoh, in his account, is as
sentimental as Tonio Kröger and almost as labile as Hanno
Buddenbrook; but he is also the religious genius who devotes his life to the attempt to replace the harsh, national-

111

istic cult of Ammon by a monotheistic, universal, far more spiritual religion of love, associated with another sun god, Aton or Aten. Joseph has the theological background to understand Ikhnaton's concepts and the sagacity to realize his weakness: Pharaoh is "on the right road but not the right man for the road." In any case, Ikhnaton, being at least fourteen centuries ahead of his time, would have been a "marked man"; but since he is, at least in Mann's version, nervous, lachrymose, and given to trances, he is doubly stigmatized. Mann has made only one really radical departure from the accepted view of Ikhnaton's religious policy: while he notes his intolerance towards the older religions, he gives no idea of its virulence, which eventually ruined Ikhnaton's reign. To have done so, of course, would have clouded the cheerful atmosphere of the story. Both Ikhnaton's rather sentimental panentheism and his amazing cosmopolitanism appear in a brief quotation from the longer of the Amarna "Hymns to Aton," sometimes attributed to Ikhnaton himself:

> The chick in the egg chirpeth in the shell, for thou givest it breath therein to sustain its life. Thou makest for it its strength in the egg in order to break it. It cometh forth from the egg to chirp . . . How much is there that thou hast made, and that is hidden from me, thou sole god, to whom none is to be likened! . . .
>
> The lands of Syria and Nubia, and the land of Egypt—thou puttest every man in his place and thou suppliest their needs.

Mann has woven phrases from this poem into Pharaoh's conversation; in *Lotte in Weimar* he uses the same process on a far greater scale in constructing Goethe's conversations and the interior monologue of the seventh chapter.

Like a skilled psychoanalyst, Joseph tries to make Pharaoh think that he has interpreted his own dreams of the cattle and the ears of corn. Proceeding *suaviter in modo, fortiter in re,* Joseph combines flattery with frankness and is not afraid to remind the unworldly Ikhnaton that "the peace of God has strong hands." The good society must be strong, and Joseph proceeds to build up a welfare state on the grand scale. It is typical of the "mediator" Joseph that his economic dictatorship is an adroit combination of capitalism and socialism. In his attack on the power of the Egyptian barons, his solicitude for the poor, his popularity, and his happy blending of cunning and benevolence, Joseph "is" Franklin Roosevelt, mythically speaking.

With the dispatch of the ten brethren to Egypt, during the seven years of famine, the reference of the novel shifts from the twentieth century back to the age of the patriarchs. The great recognition scene, one of the high points of the whole work, unites irony with tenderness. Joseph plays a benign cat-and-mouse game with his brothers and finally demands that they leave Benjamin with him in Egypt when they return to Jacob. This would all too clearly "repeat" their betrayal of Joseph himself; it had indeed been foreseen by Jacob. In a magnificent speech, Judah offers himself as a hostage instead, and under the stress of the moment confesses their full guilt, for which he is ready to atone. He has achieved a psychological "break-through," and Joseph must now reveal his identity: "Don't you see, it's I. I am your brother Joseph, of course." "It is I" was the formula in which Joseph had formerly implied his association with divine figures, but he uses it here in a purely human sense. He has given up his mythical pretensions to superhuman status; his boyish dream of pre-eminence prophesied only secular glory, for he is "no messenger of divine salvation but only an economist." After his installation as Pharaoh's minister, he had relinquished the "mythical" name Osarsiph.

Joseph's recognition of his own limitations is the final mark of his maturity; in the tradition of the Goethean *Bildungsroman,* he has renounced. In effect, he has thus forgone the tribal blessing, which is reserved for "God's heroes," prophets like Abraham, Isaac, and Jacob. God has both raised him up and rejected him, as Jacob tells him in the moving chapter "Of Withholding Love":

> You are blessed . . . from Heaven above and the depths below, blessed with gladness and destiny, with wit and with dreams. But it is a worldly blessing, not a spiritual one.

Joseph's own blessing is no mean thing: he represents the highest human synthesis of nature and spirit, rationality and intuition. In him the painful dualism of Mann's earlier heroes has been transcended. It has been pointed out that he is "the artist as leader," an artist in human affairs, and Mann often associates him with Goethe, to him another bearer of the secular blessing. Yet Joseph after all has become partially alienated from the traditions of his people and even from God. In a sense, he will always remain in the pit. His practical genius has saved his people: without it, the bearers of the spiritual blessing would have perished. "After all, bread there has to be. First comes bread and then the hosannas." But, as Mann had long before remarked, "The ideal of human welfare is of the second

114

rank." Somewhat as in Eliot's *The Cocktail Party,* the worldly ideal is subordinated to the spiritual. But the paradox remains that the secular, "humanistic" synthesis is more in accordance with Mann's thought and with the whole direction of the novel than is the austere magnificence of the religious life.

Fully to understand why Joseph, for all his brilliance, is "of the second rank," we must turn back to his father, whose figure dominates most of the first two volumes, and with whose death the tetralogy closes. Just as Joseph is the hero of the human action, Jacob, who wrestled with the angel, is the main protagonist in the divine action. Jacob is a far more archaic figure than his son, and the mythic nimbus surrounding him is more genuine. One agrees with Willa Cather that he is the more impressive figure of the two:

> Had not Jacob been there to recognize and to foresee, to be destroyed by grief and raised up again, the story of Joseph would lose its highest value . . . Take Jacob out of the history of Joseph, and it becomes simply the story of young genius; its cruel discipline, its ultimate triumph and worldly success.

Jacob's overriding concern is to contribute, after the manner of Abraham, to "laboring at the divine," in other words, to the realization and purification of God. His great illuminations come through suffering: thus Rachel's death, precisely because it is incomprehensible, teaches him that it is false to try to bind the divine powers by human wishes. His basic spirituality gives him a tragic stature from which his emotional softness, physical cowardice, and cunning do not essentially detract. In his youth, Jacob behaved if anything less "ethically" than Joseph, but he is never really the rogue Hermes; rather, a prophet whose human weaknesses are irrelevant. His hard decision to withhold the blessing of Israel from Joseph saves the novel from becoming a mere success story and is the final testimony to his own greatness.

The blessing passes then not to the wonder-child Joseph but to the problematic Judah. This son of Leah, a passionate and unhappy "slave of Astarte," is oppressed by a burning sense of guilt. But "guilt creates spirit," says Mann—clearly it did so in Jacob's case—and one has the feeling that he will be a worthy bearer of the blessing, though hardly of the stature of Jacob or Abraham. To his account of Judah Mann has connected the novella of Tamar, in line with his technique, in his mature works, of introducing tension by a strong emphasis on the erotic. Besides Tamar and Mut, there are the Negro concubine in *The Tables of the Law,* Sita in *The Transposed Heads,* and the bizarre episode of Heinz Klöpfgeissel in *Doctor Faustus.*

With a certain ironic reverence, Mann traces God's evolution as well as Joseph's. He creates man but the prophets help to create Him: a truly reciprocal relationship. Thus Abraham, who first hit upon the idea of a non-material God, is "to a certain extent" God's father. Before Abraham, the Hebrew God had been a malicious desert cobold called Yahu, more demonic than divine. Thanks to the prophets, however, he was destined for a "great theological career," as Mann puts it in one of his Voltairean moments. God progresses largely through the process of substitution, of which the replacement of Isaac by the sacrificial ram is the classic example. Thus Jacob, believing that God has slain his son, complains quite logically that He has "not kept in step." How much God owed to man is evident if one considers the fate of the Egyptian Aton. Ikhnaton's deity was clearly superior to Jehovah in some respects, but since he lacked the assistance of strong men he had no immediate future. The God of Abraham and Jacob, however, "has a future." He is so dynamic, as we learn in the "Prelude in the Upper Circles," that He is planning to sacrifice His universality by incorporating Himself in a chosen people, for the sake of becoming more thoroughly alive. Eventually He will rise again in Christianity from the pit of a nationalistic religion. It is clear, however, from the tone of *Joseph* that Mann's God is developing towards a goal more humanistic than dogmatically Christian. God is discussed, especially in the veiled criticisms of the jealous angels, with a genial irony reminiscent of Goethe's "Prologue in Heaven" in *Faust*.

In order to humanize the myth, Mann uses a variety of techniques. Perhaps the most striking is the employment of a very sophisticated psychology. Repeatedly, the "real," unconscious motives are played off against the conscious ones, as in the account of Isaac's convenient blindness when it was necessary for him to "mistake" Jacob for Esau. "Freudian slips" are introduced, and Potiphar's feelings of love and hatred towards his wife supply a convincing example of ambivalence. The part played by dreams, already a decisive one in Genesis, is greatly expanded. Broadly speaking, Mann applies his twentieth-century psychology tactfully. One is not uncomfortably aware of his sources, and when a sense of anachronism does occasionally arise, it is amusing rather than disturbing. Often the result is to make credible an incident which would otherwise be only bizarre: thus Jacob's plan to descend into the underworld, in the guise of Ishtar, to rescue his "true son" is motivated psychologically as well as mythically.

Throughout, Mann's perspective on his material is a double one. While he aims at times at the conventional suspension of disbelief, at others he accepts and revels in the task of commentator. The intention would seem to be to make us simultaneously aware of the mythical or historical past, of our own position in time, and of the interval between the two: to create in other words a polyphonic effect. Generally, a mildly ironic effect is produced, but occasionally the commentary corrodes the traditional account. Mann describes how the dying Isaac identified himself with a ram, and concludes: "Then he bleated once more, in a very natural way, and expired." He is attracted also to half-serious scholarly discussion and exegesis for their own sake, and spends many pages in treating details of the Biblical text or of one of his other sources. These very self-conscious expatiations can be amusing but become wearying as the novel approaches its end. In *Joseph the Provider*, for instance, Mann devotes several pages to the question of the exact number of Israelites whom Jacob led down into Egypt.

Another modern, and so to speak anti-mythical element lies in the various references to the contemporary scene. Merely to have chosen a Jewish subject, in the decade of Hitler's rise to power, was in itself a protest against German nationalism, but Mann in no sense means to replace one nationalism by another. *Joseph the Provider*, written under "the Egyptian sky of California," has a certain American atmosphere; *Joseph in Egypt,* in its comments on Egyptian chauvinism, is an indirect satirization of Germany, though its account of immigrants passing through the "Fortress Zel" seems to owe something to Ellis Island. When Joseph remarks that bread comes before hosannas, one is doubtless intended to recall the famous Marxist line of Bertolt Brecht:

Erst kommt das Fressen, dann kommt die Moral.

But the most important factor in Mann's reinterpretation of the myth is, of course, the way in which he changes its direction from the archaic past to the future, by his surprisingly optimistic emphasis on the idea of progress.

Joseph is the most charming, and perhaps the wisest, of Mann's longer works. Various criticisms leveled against it: undue deliberateness of pace, excessive display of erudition, Wagnerian repetitiousness, and so on, can be summed up in the charge that the novel betrays that decrease in intensity often characteristic of aging writers. At the very least, exceptions would have to be made for *The Tales of Jacob* and the high points of the final volume. On this score the most incisive critic of the novel is Mann himself. In an entry in his diary, he remarks that *Joseph* may be a "late" work both in his own career and in the history of German literature; that it may give the effect of Alexandrian artificiality. It is indeed, like much of Joyce and Eliot, often Alexandrian in manner, but it is oriented towards the future. The essential intention of *Joseph and His Brothers* is a moral one; the ironies of the work do not conceal its unabashed didacticism. Joseph, shorn of his supernatural nimbus, becomes a mythic figure in another sense: he represents a timeless human norm. In uniting the "blessings of heaven above, blessings of the deep that lieth under, blessings of the breasts, and of the womb," he exemplifies the synthesis of which Hans Castorp briefly dreamed. He is no demigod but he has learned, as a man, to die and be born again.

The Tables of the Law (1943) was written for an anthology called *The Ten Commandments,* to which Sigrid Undset, Bruno Frank, and others also contributed. The purpose of the collection was to vindicate the moral law against Fascist nihilism. In such enterprises, however laudably intended, desire generally outruns performance, but Mann's occasional piece is a brilliant improvisation. It moves in the sphere of *Joseph,* but the style is very different, the tempo far more rapid.

Mann's Moses, like Judah, longs for purity because he is sensual; above all he desires to establish a fixed moral order because the circumstances of his own life are highly irregular. Freud, like others before him, had maintained that Moses was an Egyptian. It is typical of Mann's mediating and conciliatory role that he makes his protagonist half Egyptian, half Hebrew, and this situation gives Moses the necessary "distance" from the Jews which enables him to shape them into a people. For Moses is an artist, the prophet as sculptor; Mann has modeled him largely after Michelangelo.

Throughout, Mann has kept a more consistently "modern" point of view than in *Joseph.* He explains the supernatural elements of the Biblical legend rationalistically, and includes a perhaps excessive amount of contemporary reference. The Jews who dance around the golden calf become a symbol of the deluded Germans; Moses, who first chastises them and then secures God's forgiveness, speaks for Mann himself. The story is a successful *tour de force* but not one of Mann's important novellas. It is propaganda of the better sort.

Lotte in Weimar (1939) is the longest of the various intercalated works which Mann completed during the composition of *Joseph*. The "Goethe novel" does not represent a radical shift in the direction of Mann's development: it too is a fusion of psychology and myth. Of course, in *Lotte* the historical element is far greater: in dealing with the Weimar of 1816, Mann had at his disposal an enormous mass of documentation. Mann, who is no mean Goethe scholar, absorbed countless details of the poet's life and work, but the sheer bulk of raw material was not to prove an unmixed blessing.

Much of the allusiveness of *Lotte* is lost in translation. Hundreds if not thousands of reminiscences of Goethe's lyrics, of *Faust* and other works, of his letters and conversations, have been woven into the novel, often in direct quotation, sometimes varied. Even if one catches an allusion in the English version to one of Goethe's poems, its luminosity is lost. A second difficulty is perhaps a less obvious one. Goethe's personality dominates the imagination of cultivated Germans in a way which can hardly be comprehended in other countries. It is as if Shakspere had lived only a century or so ago, as if we had had no Chaucer nor Milton to share his glory, and as if some-

121

thing approaching a religion had been based on his life as well as his works. When Mann remarks that German schoolboys learn Goethe's amours by heart like those of Zeus, he is not exaggerating: Goethe has become a myth. The *imitatio Goethe* is a real force in German intellectual life. While Mann's portrait of Goethe owes nothing to vulgar hero-worship, his novel seems to presuppose the cult of Goethe as a *Gestalt,* which goes far beyond admiration of his works as such.

Yet the success of *Lotte* in this country is not, after all, surprising. The title of the American version, *The Beloved Returns,* shows admirable intellectual tact: it implies the general human appeal of the situation, as well as the subtler mythic pattern which gradually emerges. And even if the reader does not perceive the nimbus of the "culture hero," he can regard Goethe as another paradigm of the artist: the poet not as outcast but as a figure of state, holding a position in his little duchy not dissimilar to Joseph's in Egypt.

In human terms, the novel deals with the visit to Weimar of Charlotte Buff Kestner, forty-four years after the love affair which the European success of *Werther* had made a matter of common knowledge. In Mann's account, she has been distressed not by the notoriety which Goethe's novel had forced upon her but by a far more essential injury. Goethe's love for her had not been "serious": he had made no attempt to take her away from her fiancé but had exploited the emotions of the persons involved for his own aesthetic ends. Mann's Lotte (here he has idealized the historical Charlotte) must come to terms with this experience before she can become reconciled with Goethe or with her own role. With that goal she has come to Weimar, displaying the same resoluteness which had enabled her to fulfill her middle-class destiny with her unremarkable fiancé, despite the ambiguous attentions of the poet. She had firmly dismissed the thought that things might have turned out differently; but now, as a widow, the mother of nine children, she is free to return, to try to recapture the past so that she may reinterpret it. Her feelings combine rather pathetically a sense of hurt, pride in her position in Goethe's life, and jealousy of the other women who have played a part in it.

The novel is concerned with Goethe even more than with Lotte, but for six chapters he does not directly appear in it. Instead, Mann conducts us through a series of concentric circles surrounding Goethe, until at last we arrive at the center. In a succession of conversations all concerned with the poet, the impact of a genius on his surroundings is very gradually made clear. It appears that this effect, in the case of people close to him, is a searing one: Lotte becomes aware of the odor of human sacrifice. Goethe's secretary, Riemer, who has given up a promising career to become little more than an amanuensis, has been reduced to a state of pathological ambivalence, which Mann renders with especial skill. His son August, whose personality is a caricature of his father's, has suffered still more. The poet's satellites even speak, involuntarily, in the stiffly formal style of his own old age.

At long last, in an interior monologue, Goethe himself is heard. The intention of this *tour de force* is less to furnish a dialectical reply to the accusations which have been made than to give a sort of motion picture of the poet's flow of consciousness. Mann's task is harder than Joyce's —Goethe being a somewhat more complex figure than Molly Bloom—but Mann has achieved a remarkable degree of success. It is a fascinating reconstruction, but one remains conscious of *impedimenta,* of cleverly manipulated source materials, for the monologue is largely a mosaic composed of bits and pieces of Goethe's works. As one would expect, Mann manages to indicate the range and scope of Goethe's mind far better than most of the academic biographers do. The poet's thoughts range from meteorology to plans for completing *Faust,* from didactic maxims to his very ambiguous feelings for Schiller, from erotic stirrings to neoclassical aesthetics. Perhaps the most striking achievement of the monologue is its success in indicating the unitary nature of Goethe's thought: his mode of seeing the most varied phenomena as parts of one great whole. Goethe's prophecy that the Germans' chauvinism will some day bring upon them the hatred of the world, and the introduction of certain Freudian ideas into his consciousness, make one aware of Mann behind the scenes. A thought of Goethe's may pass into another through a pun or similar association, somewhat in Joyce's manner. Some of these links are inevitably lost in translation, but a sequence like Napoleon—St. Helena—Helen of Troy—*Faust* is of course preserved. The monologue is an admirable interpretation of the poet, an essay on Goethe, largely by Goethe, and at the same time an integral part of the novel.

In Goethe's stream of consciousness, the pattern of mythic association emerges clearly. His latest love has involved him in a triangular situation reminiscent of the days of his passion for Lotte: the beloved has already "returned," in a far younger woman. Thus when he learns that the actual Lotte is in Weimar, his feelings are complicated rather than pleasant. Lotte, for her part, has had a similar uncanny sense of repetition: she feels that Goethe's unhappy son "is" her old lover; at the same time, she cannot help thinking of him as her own son. And the young blonde girl whom August will marry at his father's direction "is" Lotte in turn. It is all very complex and rather painful.

The sense of painfulness reaches a climax at the formal dinner which Goethe gives in Lotte's honor. Her reappearance is all too reminiscent of a return from the dead, and her wearing a girlish dress of the sort described in *Werther* is not a successful gesture. Goethe for his part appears distracted, remote, and insincere, and the relation between him and his admirers, the "toadies" as Lotte calls them, is unsavory.

A sudden reversal, Mann's own invention, dispels the aura of disillusioned bitterness. Goethe himself has sensed that the return must not end in a fiasco. Sharply challenged by Lotte, he pleads that he too has suffered and felt remorse for his "guiltless guilt." If Lotte, like many others, has been drawn like a moth to the flame, he is the candle who is equally consumed. Only the very alert reader notes at first reading that the whole scene is a hallucination; the reconciliation takes place, we belatedly realize, only in Lotte's mind.

Whether *Lotte in Weimar* is the best of Mann's minor novels or the least of his major works is an academic question. With the exception of Barker Fairley's books, it is the most interesting interpretation of Goethe written in many years. As a novel, it is excessively *meublé*, and surely more Alexandrian than *Joseph*. Even in the final scene, which is the most moving in the book, there is a jarring note. Goethe's last words are a direct quotation from his *The Elective Affinities*, to the effect that parted lovers will awake together in Heaven. That they have here, as in the original, an only half-sincere ring is possibly in accord with Mann's intention; but the literal quotation reminds us all too sharply that the speech is a *montage. Lotte in Weimar* is a noble experiment, an interesting operation in the borderland between fiction and biography.

While *Lotte* is important, at least as a further attempt to extend the frontiers of the novel, the long novella *The Transposed Heads* (1940) is, in Mann's words, "a metaphysical jest." One should never explain jokes, at least not at length. In Mann's adaptation of a Hindu legend, two youths, Shridaman and Nanda, represent the familiar dichotomy of spirit and life. The attractive and highly sexed Sita (who would seem to represent beauty), a young woman loved by both of them, through a most drastic Freudian slip transposes their heads so that the head of "spirit" comes to rest on the shoulders of "life," and *vice versa;* but things do not turn out as she had expected. A synthesis cannot be attained by arbitrary combinations, for "love has to do with the whole." Sita and the two youths perish, but her intelligent son, who embodies a true fusion, survives, destined for an admirable career. *The Transposed Heads* is written with verve and wit, and makes adroit use of erotic and satiric elements. Essentially it is a "finger exercise," another variation on the dualistic theme which has obsessed Mann all his life.

The bulk of *Joseph,* and of course *Lotte* and *The Transposed Heads* as well, were the products of Mann's exile. The cheerfulness of all these works, written in an apocalyptic decade, is astounding, even though Mann had an outlet in his political essays for his reactions to the time. In *Doctor Faustus* (1947) Mann returned to the present and to the theme of Germany. This amazing book was written during the years when Germany was being destroyed, but his pessimism has less obvious grounds. Nor was it based merely on the conviction that the ruin of his former country was the inevitable result of its contemporary crimes; he had come to believe that strains of spiritual arrogance, long inherent in the German tradition, were ultimately responsible. Not that he could render judgment in remote serenity: he was himself a part of that tradition. "Where I am, there is Germany," he had remarked, early in his exile. In his testimony on German culture, Mann is the accused as well as the accuser.

7. EXILE'S RETURN

IN *Doctor Faustus* MANN UNDERTOOK HIS MOST ONEROUS task: to represent in symbolic form the decline and eventual ruin of Germany. No colors could seem too black to represent the moral, political, and cultural catastrophe; for it should not be forgotten that Mann is relating the fall of his own nation, of a tradition which, despite all reservations and ambiguities, he loves.

Not surprisingly, *Doctor Faustus* has acquired a reputation for complexity and difficulty. Yet the central conception of the novel, the close association of Germany, music, and the Faustian tradition, is persuasive, well-conceived, and relatively simple. The composer Adrian Leverkühn, Mann's "Faustus," is linked to Germany, a "Faustian" nation in Spengler's sense, primarily through music; and music Mann of course considers a perilously fascinating force, associated with political backwardness and the cult of the non-rational.

Inevitably, it is the original, somber tradition of the

128

chapbook Faustus to which Mann returns, for his protagonist must be damned; the optimism of Goethe, whose
Faust is saved despite various offenses, no longer seems
valid. It would be simplistic to call Mann's hero a symbol
of National Socialism. He has too much distinction, intellectual, social, and personal, for that. Yet he does share
through his coldness, his ruthlessness, his *hubris*, in the
guilt of modern Germany. The parallel is by no means
exact, but it exists.

Only a few of the innumerable analogues and cross-
references, so to speak, through which Mann tries to
show the unity of his "grand design" can be cited. Many
links connect Adrian to the traditional Faustus: his early
interest in theology; the pact with the Devil, which gives
him twenty-four years of heightened genius; the allusion
to the magic cloak that carried Faustus through the air;
the bathysphere and the interest in physics, correspond-
ing to Faustus' titanic desire to master all knowledge.
Like his archetype, Adrian cannot marry or love without
the most disastrous consequences; and his final meeting
with his friends at his Bavarian retreat—perhaps the most
powerful scene in the novel—recalls Faustus' farewell to
his companions both in language and in details of the
action. Even such an apparently trivial detail as Adrian's
control over the dog Kaschperl reminds one of Faustus'
friendly relations with the black poodle; and Kaschperl,
in his turn, bears one of the nicknames of the Devil.

Germany also "is" Faustus; to gain its ends, it has signed
a pact in blood. At the end of the War it is dashed into
the abyss, "in the grasp of demons." Long before, it has
become evident that the nation has sold its soul.

Thus in Mann's rather complicated equation, Adrian is himself obviously a symbol of Germany. Zeitblom, the narrator, draws a "symbolic parallel" between one of the composer's attacks of illness and the hectic condition of his country after 1918. At times, the deliberate rebarbarization of German culture is paralleled in Adrian's work. His "Apocalipsis cum figuris" is "streamlined"—Mann, perhaps influenced by the neo-barbarism of Hollywood, uses the American term; the composition, like the theories of the Nazis, gives an effect of "exploding old-fashionedness." Just as Faust, even in Goethe, has something Mephistophelean in his nature, both Adrian and Germany are Satanic as well as Faustian. The concept of "breaking through," one of the central themes of the whole work, applies equally to the German thrust for world power and to Adrian's desperate efforts to create a new music.

Fundamentally there is only one problem in the world, and it has this name. How does one break through? How does one emerge into the open air? How does one burst the chrysalis and become a butterfly?

It is Adrian speaking. Like Germany, he has come late upon the historical scene; he is willing to pay any price to break the old pattern and set up his own. His final collapse is described at the time when the Allied armies are overrunning Germany. In the final sentence of the novel, Zeitblom's words: "God have mercy on your poor soul, my friend, my fatherland" reassert the fundamental parallel with the finality of a great chord.

Yet it is not enough to say that Adrian is the modern

Faustus and modern Germany. He is also the artist, a
sort of Tonio Kröger in reverse, who does not regret his
isolation, but looks down with cold contempt on the
bourgeois and the ordinary. As artist, he is associated,
more or less closely, with a variety of other figures. Most
obviously, he recalls Nietzsche, particularly in his isolation,
his wilful contracting of a venereal disease which eventually causes insanity, his tragicomic proposal of marriage,
and his pride. To some extent he is linked with Beethoven,
another "Faustian" musician whose late works went beyond the limits of his contemporaries' understanding.
Adrian is reminiscent, in different ways, of certain more
recent German composers: Schönberg with his twelve-
tone scale, Mahler, especially in his Tenth Symphony,*

* Compare some of the memoranda for this work:

3RD MOVEMENT (PURGATORIO)

Page 4: *Death! Transfiguration!*
Page 3: *COMPASSION!*
   O God! O God, why hast thou forsaken me?

4TH MOVEMENT

The Devil leads me in a dance
Madness seizes me, Accursed!
Demolish me that I may forget my being!
That I may cease to exist, that I may . . .

End of Movement: (Completely muffled drum) *None
but you knows what it signifies!*
   Ah! Ah! Ah! Fare thee well my lyre!
   Farewell, Farewell, Farewell Ah well—Ah Ah

(Quoted in Alma Mahler [Werfel], *Gustav Mahler;* New York:
Viking, 1946, p. 277.) Gustav Mahler was one of the prototypes
of another isolated genius, Gustave von Aschenbach. For other points
in Mahler's life and work which suggest analogies to Adrian, see pp.
123 and 177 of Mrs. Werfel's book. This does not mean of course

and Hugo Wolf, whose tortured career ended in madness. Broadly speaking, he stands for the "late" artist, who must make an enormous effort to achieve originality. "Certain things are no longer possible," says Mann's Devil, who seems to have read Spengler. And finally, Adrian represents one side, the "daemonic," largely suppressed aspect of Mann himself. Her father, Monika Mann tells us, is obsessed by music, and is afraid of it. Various autobiographical details support the view that Adrian "is" one aspect of Mann; even the development of his works, from the impressionistic through the parodistic to the tragic, is parallel to the author's. It can even be argued that he represents what the author himself might have become, if he had not turned away from some of the tendencies of earlier years. Certain lines of thought in the *Reflections of a Non-Political Man,* had they been consistently followed, would have led him to share in the ruin which overtook his protagonist.

In the attempt to unify a work of such complexity of theme and variety of associations, Mann was faced by no mean problem. On first consideration, the vast bulk of *Doctor Faustus* appears inchoate, but its structure is actually highly elaborate. As in so many of his other works, Mann inclines, in *Doctor Faustus,* towards a musical form; in his latest novel he builds up the themes first sounded early in the work with particular care. In the brief first chapter, to cite a single example, many of the important themes are introduced: the nature of genius

that Adrian "is" Mahler, any more than he is a portrait of Schönberg or Wolf; like so many of Mann's major figures, he is drawn from many models but "is" only himself.

and its affinity to the "daemonic"; the "horrible pact" (not to be signed until the center of the novel); the proud isolation of the hero; and his inhuman coldness. All of these themes, above all the last, are treated as leitmotifs and recur again and again. Mann varies the tempo of his work quite as consciously and boldly as a composer might; he is audacious enough to begin with a protracted *ritardando*. Only very gradually, the novel builds up to a tremendous *prestissimo* at the end. Certain episodes, like the story of Inez or of Echo, have a mood or "key" of their own, very different from that of the "symphony" in general. I do not imply that Mann has followed any musical form in slavish detail; but merely that, broadly speaking, the novel may be called symphonic.

Structurally, *Doctor Faustus* seems to be composed of several long movements. The first section is devoted to exposition in the conventional sense, and includes as well the first assertion of the major themes: the magical, music, Hetaera Esmeralda, and the medieval, with associations of the diabolical and of mass hysteria. Another major block centers largely on Adrian's musical and intellectual education; here too the diabolic and the political strains are especially emphasized. This section culminates in the two cardinal experiences of Adrian's life, his decision to become a musician and his surrender to disease (presumably because he knows subconsciously that the infection will heighten his genius). The embrace of Hetaera Esmeralda is the real pact with the Devil; the dialogue only serves as a formal ratification. In the precise center of the novel stands Mann's *tour de force*, the dialogue with the Devil. Its effects are evident in the increasing "daemonism" of the work from that point on: in politics, a clearer drift towards Fascism; in Adrian's work, an alternation between periods of furious productivity and miserable illness; in the life of his Munich acquaintances, an increasing degeneration. Also, since Adrian has passed the peak of his life, events in his descent tend to parallel those of the ascent: thus the farm in Bavaria repeats his boyhood home; the Kridwiss circle takes up and exaggerates the non-rational politics of the students at Halle. Along with the increasing strain of diabolism in Adrian and in German society, the dominant theme of "breakthrough at any price" is developed. Then a succession of chapters deals with the partial "rally" of Adrian and Germany; it is the period of the relatively good days of the German Republic, and Leverkühn seems to be attaining a degree of health and even of human warmth. Sinister notes are of course included; the recovery of the 1920's was precarious and ambiguous. The final section is one of catastrophe. Adrian's attempts to love result in disaster: he becomes in effect the murderer of his ambiguous friend Rudi Schwerdtfeger. The death of the idolized child Echo drives him to "take back" the Ninth Symphony; in other words, to repudiate the ideals on which the culture of Germany's classical age had been built. As throughout, the comments of Serenus Zeitblom on the progress of the Second World War provide a sort of counterpoint; here they reflect the annihilating defeat of 1945 and the burning shame of the German nation. After the farewell to his friends (closely patterned after the chapbook) Adrian falls into utter madness. Yet he has produced his last, presumably his greatest work during this time, "The

Lamentation of Dr. Faustus," a work free of parody, the expression of despair and yet of a final transcendent hope. A "postscript" by Serenus closes the frame of the work.

Whether one accepts the supernatural element as objectively real or considers the manifestations of the infernal as a series of hallucinations produced by Adrian's disease, makes very little difference in the effect of the novel, and Mann leaves the level of interpretation up to the reader. Whether Leverkühn's inability to love, for instance, is attributed to the terms of the pact or explained psychologically, hardly matters.

The manipulation of time shows the virtuosity that one would expect from the author of *The Magic Mountain*. Zeitblom writes his account from 1943 to 1945, while Adrian's years of sanity extend from 1885 to 1930; he dies ten years later. A long chain of political insets, many of which approach the lapidary form of the communiqué, draw the two times together. More significantly: Zeitblom's description of Adrian's final breakdown is directly linked to his account of the death agonies of the Third Reich; thus the two catastrophes, separated by fifteen years, fuse into one in the mind of the reader.

From another point of view, *Doctor Faustus* can be regarded as the *summa* ("synthesis" would be too optimistic a term) of themes which Mann has treated in other works. It is characteristic that here he carries them to new extremes. Thus Adrian is the sick artist, but his illness is not the vague and somehow romantic debility of the decadent; he does not suffer from tuberculosis, a relatively "poetic" disease, but from syphilis. Again, as in *The Magic Mountain*, disease serves to intensify talent or genius; again, it is closely linked to love—but "love" is represented not by the agreeably exotic Clavdia, but by a prostitute. Adrian is the isolated artist but in this work without any sentimental longing for the bourgeois sphere, which he scorns with frigid pride.

Mann's passion for music had often been expressed elsewhere, most notably in *Buddenbrooks, Tristan,* and in the interpretations of Hans Castorp's favorite gramophone records; but nowhere so intensively and extensively. Obsessed as he is by the belief that music is the realm of danger and death, perhaps even of the diabolic, Mann naturally makes his Faustus a musician. The theme of music is increasingly developed: in the part-songs which Hanne, the stall-maid, teaches to Adrian and Serenus; in the eccentric but memorable effusions of Kretzschmar; and most strikingly in Mann's many reproductions of compositions both real and imaginary. These are far more ambitious, more frequent, and more "professional" than anything Mann has attempted before. No longer does he try primarily to interpret the ideas and emotions associated with a given work, as in *Buddenbrooks,* for example; here the central aim is to render in words the effect of music *as music.* This is perhaps an impossible task, and one is reminded of the metaphor of the deep-sea diver who ventures more and more boldly until the final descent from which he does not return. Be that as it may, *Doctor Faustus,* in this regard as in many others, would seem to mark the *non plus ultra* of Mann's career. That music is an anti-bourgeois, anti-political force is a conceit long familiar to Mann's readers, but only here is it clearly implied that this aspect of music is also deplorable.

As in most of **Mann's** novels, there is in *Doctor Faustus*
a great deal of thinly veiled self-depiction and self-
criticism, also of commentary on his earlier works. Thus
when we hear that Wagner created, in the leitmotif, an
"apparatus of significant simultaneity"; that Adrian loves
to characterize things and persons by a brief allusion; that
he is fond of "indirections, intellectual tricks, and ironies,"
the reference to the author is clear enough. Adrian's remark

> The Germans have a two-track mind and an inexcusable
> habit of combination; they always want one thing and another,
> they want to have it both ways. They are capable of turning
> out great personalities with antithetic principles of thought
> and life.

is obviously reminiscent of Mann's own mode of thought.

Besides the lavish use of parallels, some subtly, some
obviously drawn, which align the political, musical, and
personal directions of *Doctor Faustus,* Mann employs the
familiar technique of the leitmotif to give unity and shape
to his novel. As in *Joseph,* the leitmotif of repeated situation or character is more important than the reiteration
of a given phrase or word, and the concept of eternal recurrence is used to give the sense of a mysteriously pre-
determined pattern. The farm in Bavaria where Adrian
spends his last two years has an uncanny resemblance to
his ancestral home in central Germany; the "mother
figure," the slovenly maid, the dog, and so on, all reap-
pear, slightly varied. One can even speak of a sort of recurrence in style. Mann's occasional use of a modified
sixteenth-century German, with Faustian, Lutheran, and
diabolic associations, is not primarily a device to cre-

137

ate "atmosphere." Rather, it too tends to interrelate characters: the grotesque theologian Kumpf, Adrian, and the Devil all express themselves in this idiom at one time or another.

As in *Death in Venice*, Mann gains a sinister effect by introducing, under various disguises, the same evil character. Thus Eberhard Schleppfuss ("Dragfoot": his name implies the limping devil of tradition), a specialist in the psychology of religion, is clearly a "devil" character, though he also recalls both Krokowski and Naphta of *The Magic Mountain*. The pimp who guides Adrian to the brothel in Leipzig has a certain resemblance to Schleppfuss, as does the Devil himself, who in one of the forms in which he appears to Adrian, wears the "little, parted beard" affected by that unprepossessing instructor. Another link is the use of the infernal color to connect the Leipzig pander in his red cap with the Devil in his two other incarnations—as a tough customer with reddish hair and blood-shot eyes, and as a music critic [!], whose eyes are likewise reddened.

Another, much subtler identification has been argued by Mr. Victor Oswald in a brilliant paper. Hetaera Esmeralda, he believes, is none other than the rich Hungarian noblewoman Frau von Tolna, in the novel a rather shadowy figure, the patroness of Adrian. Mr. Oswald's argument is persuasive, if highly complicated, and if one accepts his identification of the two figures, the novel gains greatly in emotional immediacy and power; Esmeralda, a rather attractive figure in her own right, attains a certain tragic stature.

These are but a few of many devices. Mann is fond of

citing Heine's symbol of the gigantic tapestry to characterize his later novels. One might equally well refer to the image of the loom, which Goethe uses in describing the workings of the mind:

> Where a thousand threads one treadle shows,
> Where fly the shuttles hither and thither.
> Unseen the threads are knit together,
> And an infinite combination grows.

Similarly, in Mann's concept of the integrated, musical novel, every important action or character is intricately related to a host of others; one treadle moves, if not a thousand threads, several or all of the important strands.

Clearly, it is the political element which accounts for the degree of pessimism in *Doctor Faustus*. This is a desperately serious book, written *de profundis*. The problem of the German, the *malheur d'être allemand*, is discussed once more, but here there is only a paradoxical hope of an ultimate solution. The almost complete despair about Germany goes beyond the bitter condemnations which Goethe and Hölderlin, Heine and Nietzsche expressed in their blackest moments. Mann's sense of guilt is so deep and so inclusive that he senses a diabolic, almost Nazi strain in the greatest Germans:

Was not this [Nazi] reign, in its words and deeds, only the distorted, vulgarized, hideous realization of a frame of mind and manner of judging the world, to which one must concede genuineness of character and which the man of Christian-humanistic stamp, not without fear, finds expressed in the features of our great men, the most powerful embodiments of the German spirit?

It is Zeitblom speaking of course, but it is obvious enough from the novel and from certain of the later essays that

139

he speaks for Mann. German culture and German tradition are polluted, retroactively as it were, by Nazism; and Mann, the greatest living heir of the tradition, views it at times almost from the point of view of Lord Vansittart. Yet there are hints of definite though muted hope despite the catastrophe:

> . . . grant that expressiveness—expression as lament—is the issue of the whole construction [Adrian's last work]: then may we not parallel with it another, a religious one, and say too (though only in the lowest whisper) that out of the sheerly irremediable, hope might germinate? It would be but a hope beyond hopelessness, the transcendence of despair—not its betrayal, but the miracle that passes belief.

The question "What is German?", treated with a rather optimistic irony in *The Magic Mountain,* now finds a simple answer: after Dachau and Buchenwald, to be German is to be damned. And yet—with Mann there is always a "yet"—this is a profoundly German book, a symbolic exile's return from Egypt and India, the confession of an agonized (and at least in part, an unrequited) love for Germany. The American citizen, champion of democratic socialism and of a new humanism, the admirer of Franklin Roosevelt, cannot after all completely repudiate his own tradition.

To say, as one must, that this is primarily a book for Germans, does not deny it universality. Adrian's quandary is that of any intelligent artist or of an intellectual in any field in a "late" age, sensitive of the achievement of the past and of the weight of tradition. Scornful of mere virtuosity and convinced that the inherited forms have in large degree become obsolete, he realizes the difficulty of original creation and the necessity for the boldest experiments. His predicament is essentially the same as that of Joyce and Eliot, and of the late Mann himself. He finds that the old pattern has been outworn, but that it is enormously difficult to shape a new one; to do so, he is ready to sell his soul. For to refuse to make the pact with the Devil would have been the betrayal of his genius: there could have been no "break-through," and his great works would never have been written. Further: the Devil tells him that future generations will draw health from the products of his illness; and Mann's Devil, it is emphasized, is no liar. In this perspective, Adrian's decision appears as a heroic one. He is in fact sacrificing himself for the sake of the future, and one can almost speak of vicarious atonement.

So much then for Mann's intention; it is on his execution that controversy is likely to center for a long time. There is a great wealth in *Doctor Faustus;* also, there is a great deal to discourage the casual reader. Quite aside from the impossibility of rendering adequately in English this extremely "German" work, there are obvious charges which have been laid, not without justice: in parts of the novel a bookish, almost pedantic tone, garrulousness, extreme slowness of movement, and a resulting lack of emotional force. (That these characteristics are in harmony with the character of Zeitblom, the narrator, does not make them any more exciting.) It has also been argued that the main characters, Adrian above all, are burdened with such a weight of symbolic meanings that they do not really "live."

The most obvious objection deals with the length and

number of the episodes and apparent digressions. Most
or all of these can be shown to have a relationship to the
central theme, but whether all of them become organic
parts of the whole, or have sufficient vividness to be justified on their own merits, is indeed another question. And
even if each excursus were defensible in itself—which I
do not believe to be the case—the sum total would still
seem to be too great.

In the complex structure of *Doctor Faustus,* some of the
episodes have more than a single function, but most of
them are related to one definite major motif. The discussions of Beethoven, for instance, reinforce the Faustian
theme. The interpretations of Adrian's compositions are
not of course digressions at all; they are central in the
spiritual development of the hero, and of Germany. Yet
the descriptions of the music store in Halle might well
have been cut down; and the treatment of such topics as
Beethoven's attitude towards Bach has an undeniably
professorial ring. The scientific interests of Adrian and
his father recall the titanic thirst for universal knowledge
of the Renaissance Faustus, while the account of the
butterfly collection serves as a "musical" anticipation of
Hetaera Esmeralda. In Adrian's life, his relations with
Schwerdtfeger, Marie Godeau, and Echo illuminate the
cardinal condition of the pact: he must remain cold; his
attempts to gain love lead to catastrophe.

A number of episodes reveal the decay of German society or show the growth of lines of thought which eventually converge in Nazism. Thus Baron von Gleichen-
Russwurm, a descendant of Schiller, is involved in a sordid
though rather comical crime. The unhappy lives of Clarissa

and Inez Rodde, like the strange, parasitical existence of Rudi Schwerdtfeger, exemplify the same decadence. The students at Halle, some of whom bear symbolic names like Deutschlin, von Teutleben, and Dungersheim, indulge in loose, highfalutin, pseudo-metaphysical discussion which often amounts to parlor Fascism; Professor Kumpf and *Privatdozent* Schleppfuss, at the same university, combine the pre-Nazi note with the introduction of demonology (Faustus again!) into theology. Later, in Munich, the *avant garde* participates gleefully in the "treason of the intellectuals," the unconditional surrender to irrationality and myth. Zeitblom's analysis of Germany's role in the First World War (which he defends, as Mann did at the time) also has a certain proto-Nazi aspect, and the nostalgic reference to the near-victory at the Marne reinforces the "break-through" motif. Surely the relation of some of these incidents to the central themes is so tenuous that one may speak of a weakness of the "grand design." One thinks particularly of the lives of the Rodde sisters, vividly related to be sure, but perhaps better suited to inclusion in another work.

To turn to another major accusation: Is Adrian a person, or a cluster of symbols and associations? The implied equation of genius with guilt is not necessarily convincing to those who do not accept this *idée fixe* of Mann's as axiomatic. Adrian "comes to life" mainly in the latter part of the novel; indeed, the whole work does not fully gather momentum until the central dialogue with the Devil. One important incident seems a bit forced: the reader may know of Nietzsche's apparently deliberate contraction of syphilis, and yet find Adrian's "daemonic" behavior less than credible. The line of association leads away from Adrian the human being to the historical prototype. Yet Leverkühn becomes a "real" and extraordinarily appealing person. Mann consciously avoided giving a clear description of his appearance. To have done so would have betrayed the "secret identity" of Adrian and his friend Zeitblom: the two represent the "two souls" of Mann himself.

Serenus Zeitblom then, a subtly realized figure, embodies the bourgeois, humanistic, and professorial side of the older Mann. He has been compared to Wagner, the proverbially pedantic famulus of the traditional Faustus, but the analogy is hardly just. Mann's depreciations of his intelligence are not to be taken too literally, and Zeitblom changes under the blows of circumstance. As the book goes on, his narrative style develops from a boring long-windedness to vitality and force. No longer serene, he is "knowing through sympathy," and he gains political, as well as human insight. It is clearly implied that he is politically and ethically right in his humanistic, "Western" orientation. His one, but grave offense is that he awakened too late from that non-political state which Mann had once praised as characteristic of the cultivated *Bürger* at his best. He assumes his share of the national guilt—this seems to be characteristic of those Germans who are objectively the least to blame—yet like Mann himself he feels that he, as one who stood aside during the Nazi period, is irrevocably cut off from the mass of his fellow-citizens. As so often in Mann's works, one is led back, willy-nilly, into the autobiographical. For he too, in a more literal sense, is an exile; he has undoubtedly suffered from the estrangement from his original public; and the exile's return has taken place only in the spirit, and in a partial and conditional sense.

To grant the magnificence of Mann's aim in *Doctor Faustus,* the brilliance of some of its passages, and the skilful weaving of the "gigantic tapestry" is not of course to maintain that the novel is a satisfying aesthetic whole. Comparison with the novellas would be meaningless, but among the longer works, *The Magic Mountain,* for instance, is formally more successful, and conveys a far greater sense of intellectual excitement. Like *Ulysses, Doctor Faustus* is a fantastically learned work, and its erudition is at times annoyingly obvious. Yet whatever its weaknesses, it is Thomas Mann's most moving book. Its more powerful chapters gain added force from Mann's new single-mindedness, and the use of a native legend rather than an exotic myth gives greater authenticity. Compare for example the fundamental seriousness of Mann's treatment of the Devil with the playful attitude towards Hebrew angels and Egyptian gods in *Joseph! Doctor Faustus* is an "end product"; it belongs, like the second part of Goethe's *Faust,* with vast, difficult late works which contain an enormous variety of riches.

8. PROSPERO

IN THE LAST YEARS OF HIS LIFE, THOMAS MANN REPEATEDLY quoted Prospero's line "And my ending is despair." Productive though they were, the years after *Doctor Faustus* were marked by doubts, anxieties, and tensions. It is not too much to say that Mann wrestled with a sense of despair during his last decade; he overcame it at the end, as his final works testify, but only after a protracted struggle. Like Adrian Leverkühn, he was threatened by a sense of absolute artistic nihilism.

Perhaps his disappointment with the reception accorded his *Doctor Faustus* was the prime cause of Mann's dejection. That "tragic novel," it will be recalled, was intended as his own break-through to a type of fiction which was to rival Dostoievski's in intensity and far surpass it in integrated form. When he was taken very seriously ill in 1945 while working on *Doctor Faustus*, he believed, as did some of his friends, that "the book" was responsible. Years later he affirmed that it was the work he valued most, "simply because it cost me the most of my heart's blood," and admitted that he instantly took a dislike to anyone who disliked the novel. Many, in fact, either did not like it or expressed serious reservations, and Mann was deeply wounded. However much one may deplore the violence of his reaction, it is a fact, and does much to explain the darkness of his mood.

Of course there were other factors. He was deeply disturbed by the trend of American policy and politics after the War. No Communist, he was very much the anti-anti-Communist, and feared that militant resistance to Stalinism might lead to the rebirth of Fascism, in America and elsewhere; he was particularly concerned about developments in Western Germany. Like all sensible persons, he was horrified at the prospect of atomic warfare. For his political views he was fiercely attacked, and not only by reactionaries. Politics were never Mann's real *forte*, and he was perhaps more gallant than discreet in continuing to express himself on matters of public concern once the battle against Hitler had been won. One of the by-products of Mann's exercise of his democratic rights was that he was upon occasion quoted out of context and traduced by both the McCarthyites and Stalinites. It is small wonder that he came to prefer the calm of Switzerland—where he took up residence in 1952—to life in the United States.

However depressing the atmosphere of the time, it did not decrease Mann's persistent and steady productivity; he continued to devote every morning to creative work. His *persona* Gustave von Aschenbach had wished to grow old, since in his view only that artist who is fertile in every stage of human development may be considered truly great. In the eight years which remained to him after completing *Doctor Faustus,* Mann produced two novels (*The Holy Sinner* and *Felix Krull*), the long short story *The Black Swan,* several essays, among which the two devoted to Chekhov and Schiller are particularly impressive, and a number of shorter pieces. Not every product of his old age is an unqualified success, but each bears the stamp of quality and is marked as it were with the words *Thomas Mann fecit.*

The key to Mann's *The Holy Sinner* (1951) is found in a passage in *Doctor Faustus* in which Adrian Leverkühn discusses his plan of writing an opera for marionettes, based on the naively sensational story of Pope Gregory in the *Gesta Romanorum.* In this medieval variation of the myth of Oedipus, Gregory, himself the child of incest, unknowingly commits incest with his mother; after realizing his sin, he atones for it by seventeen years of self-imposed isolation on a lonely rock, where he shrinks almost to the size of a hedgehog. Miraculously he is called to Rome; the bells peal, struck by no human hand; he becomes a "very great pope." An opera based on such a theme could, according to Leverkühn, appeal to the broad public through its piquancy and melodramatic character, while furnishing the élite with the pleasures of parody. Similarly, in the novel Mann actually wrote, the double incest shocks or titillates the general reader. At the same time, the love of brother and sister is symbolic of the attraction felt by the unique, "chosen" person towards someone as like to himself as possible. Thus seen, it is closely related to the undisguised self-love of Narcissus-figures like Felix Krull, and is an emotion appropriate to artists and "marked men" as such.

148

One recalls Siegfried and Sieglinde in *The Blood of the Walsungs*, and Huia and Tuia in *Joseph in Egypt*. Incest is all right as long as you keep it in the family, the Irish bull has it.

Largely though not entirely, Mann's novel followed Leverkühn's prescription for a puppet opera; basically it is parody. Later, to be sure, Mann wrote in a brief essay that *The Holy Sinner* preserved "with pure seriousness the religious kernel [of the legend], its Christianity, the idea of sin and of grace." It is hard though to sense "pure seriousness" when God, after Gregory has prayed the good emperor Trajan out of Hell, lets the all too kindly pope know that enough is enough; he has got away with saving the pagan, but he had better not try such tricks twice. At the end Gregory rejoices that he did not blunder into an affair with his daughters, with further incestuous results. "There are limits to everything. The world is finite." A serious element is indeed to be found, when Mann writes, in the familiar vein of the Bildungsroman, of young Gregory's dedication to the search for his own identity and role in the world. Basically, however, Mann has used the most terrible and the most sacred of themes —incest and divine grace—as counters in an aesthetic game.

Mann's tone is most obviously ironic in his treatment of the various miracles of the legend. Thus, when all the bells of Rome are supernaturally set to pealing for three days and three nights, there is a run on cotton wool, and the dealers force up the price. He explains Gregory's survival on the rock by having him lap up a nourishing liquid, secreted by the earth, which formed regularly in

149

a natural hollow; but adds that in seventeen years the sinner's body had shrunk until it was "little larger than a hedgehog's." Mock naturalism is combined with a mock miracle.

The narrative is constructed around a series of recognition scenes, which illustrate in their variety the breadth of Mann's concept of parody. When Sibylla, the wife and mother of Gregory, realizes that the truth is about to be revealed, her desperate effort to escape the inevitable by suppressing all questions recalls Jocasta's. It is Mann's parody at its most serious; the ironic touches are few, and we have escaped for a while from the world of marionettes. By contrast, when the two pious Romans, guided by a miraculous vision, find Gregory on his rock and discover that their new pope is a shrunken little beast, the tone is that of sheer burlesque. Fortunately, Gregorius regains his former size "before the end of two hours." The most daring scene is the final mutual recognition of mother and son, after Gregory has been installed at Rome. Both confess that their incest could not be excused by ignorance; the act was "conscious-unconscious," and "beneath, where truth abides in quietness, the identity had been known at the first glance." One touch of Freudianism has dispelled the seeming innocence of the medieval tale, but a benign God forgives them nevertheless.

Mann's greatest instrument in the transmutation of the legend was language. It is style, above all, which establishes his and our distance from the story, and it is style which denaturalizes it, in more senses than one. The narrator invokes as it were a super-narrator, "the spirit of story-telling," who hovers above the work, benevolent

150

but objective. This spirit, we are told, is international:

> . . . It is quite uncertain in what language I write, whether
> Latin, French, German, or Anglo-Saxon. . . . By no means
> do I assert that I possess all the tongues; but they run all to-
> gether in my writing and become one—in other words, lan-
> guage. . . . The spirit of narration is free to the point of ab-
> straction, whose medium is language in and for itself, lan-
> guage itself, which sets itself as absolute and does not greatly
> care about idioms and national linguistic gods.

In line with this belief, Mann weaves numbers of Old
French and Middle High German words into his account.
Some of them are made clear by the context; some are
not. Anglicisms abound, and there are some American-
isms as well. "Pep," for example, seems to reflect Mann's
sojourn in California. As Goethe remarked, no one walks
under the palm trees without paying a penalty for it.

Clearly, a game is being played, a sort of *Glasperlen-
spiel* or bead game, to cite the central image of Hermann
Hesse's *Magister Ludi*. It is parody for its own sake, and,
like Prokofieff's *Classical* Symphony, parody completely
devoid of bitterness. To use a phrase of Schiller's, the
form has consumed the material. One can regard *The
Holy Sinner* as comedy, as relaxation after the tragic
tensions of *Doctor Faustus*. Yet as Mann himself noted,
the skeptical smile of the narrator is a melancholy one. As
the Devil remarked to Leverkühn, the parodist cannot
expect to achieve either happiness or greatness; his art is
expressive of a certain aristocratic nihilism. Mann believed that he might well be the last of many authors to
treat the legend of Gregory, before the long night of
barbarism descended on the world.

This belief underlies *The Holy Sinner* but is not made

explicit there; the pessimism is between the lines, as it were. In *The Black Swan* (1953) it becomes obvious to the dimmest eye: this is Mann's least happy work, in both senses. The title given the translation is far too pretty: the original means "The Deceived Woman," and a sense of sour disillusion pervades this longish novella. On the literal level, the story tells of the last, literally morbid passion of a woman in her fifties and her sudden death. Rosalie von Tümmler, a sentimental, warm-blooded, very maternal woman, falls in love with Ken Keaton, a young American, who is about the age of her two children. Her situation is the more precarious because she has recently passed through the climacteric, and suffers keenly from a sense of biological inferiority. To her inexpressible joy, her vital functions are restored, or seem to be; she triumphantly compares herself to the Sarah of the Old Testament. Disregarding the warnings of her daughter, she pursues the American youth. On an excursion to a Rococo castle on the Rhine, the group encounters two black swans, obvious symbols of death. Undeterred, Rosalie declares her love, and a rendezvous is arranged, but never kept. She is suddenly struck down by cancer of the womb; what she had thought the evidence of biological renascence was actually a symptom of disease. Mann allows her a serene death: she believes that nature has dealt with her kindly, with love rather than deceit. But the reader can hardly forget the title of the story.

Very possibly there is political allegory here, as has been suggested. The young American is well-meaning but callow; his cultural enthusiasms cannot be taken too seriously; and while he seems robust, he has been rather seriously wounded in the war. It is significant that Rosalie's highly perceptive daughter, who seems to represent the younger European intellectuals, rejects the American. His influence can further only a hectic and false recovery. To translate from human to contemporary political terms: Marshall Plans will fail and Fulbright Programs are futile. Mother Europe is dying. The relation between Keaton and Rosalie is a curious parallel to the alliance between youth and age in Vladimir Nabokov's *Lolita*.

The novella displays the expected traits of parody, and others as well. In the expository sections, Mann uses a deliberately old-fashioned and sentimental prose, as if he were writing for a woman's magazine of fifty years ago. Clichés abound: flowers are the "children of the meadow" and the rose is "the queen of flowers." The sexual symbolism is surprisingly obvious, as is the treatment of the old theme of nature versus spirit. Rosalie's daughter is an artist, and of course all artists must be marked men; her stigma is a club foot. There are some admirable passages, but in others Mann has given a sleazy character to the very texture of his prose, as if implying a narrator of a very inferior sort. At its best, Mann's work is characteristically marked by a tension between affection and irony. Indeed, in *Lotte in Weimar*, Mann attributes to Goethe a definition of culture as a synthesis of parody and love. *The Black Swan* is an almost completely loveless work.

The most radical use of parody here is the turn given to Mann's once cherished concept of the *Liebestod*. Here too, love and death seem to Rosalie to be metaphysically interwoven, but in the end it all comes down to cancer.

It may be recalled that Leverkühn, in his despair, wrote a work designed to "take back" the Ninth Symphony, in other words to recant the ideals on which German humanism was founded. In *The Black Swan*, Mann takes back the ideals of German romanticism.

In a candid evaluation of *The Black Swan*, Thomas Mann calmly noted the fact that not every experiment can succeed. One of his authentic successes, *Confessions of Felix Krull, Confidence Man*, Part I (1954), followed the disappointing novella; Mann reasserted his powers most convincingly. He had begun this portrait of the artist as criminal over forty years before (see above, p. 60 f.): the specialist will be able to note some of the seams where the various sections are joined together, but the author achieved an amazing degree of unity. In any case, no one expects tight integration in a picaresque novel. What Mann has generally maintained is unity of tone. The latter parts of *Krull* reveal his increasing preoccupation with myth, and the happy hero does at times transcend his status as a rogue, but neither of these changes is disturbing; it is rather a matter of nuances.

While Mann, in the latter parts of *Krull*, was consciously following the tradition of such rogue novels as Grimmelshausen's *Simplizissimus*, his original concept of the story was rather different. In planning a study of the artist as mountebank, he drew on a book called "The Prince of Thieves," the confessions of the Roumanian swindler Manolescu, for raw material. His style is a deliberate parody of Goethe's prose. Such an intention sounds almost blasphemous to many German ears, and Mann is a bit apologetic about it, though he might have cited the poet himself in his own defense. Goethe had written, for example: ". . . the juggler and poet are the closest of kin, happily one seeks and finds the other." In Mann's view, even Goethe, even Gustave von Aschenbach, as dealers in the world of fictions, have a great deal in common with the swindler; no Olympian attitude is to be taken seriously.

Various other parallels could be cited. Mann puts many of Goethe's favorite ideas and images into Krull's mouth, even the paradoxical notion of "innate merit," the belief that some men deserve praise for virtues they were born with. Convinced that he is "carved out of finer wood" than his contemporaries, Felix remarks that it is strange, though fundamentally right, that he is praised for his inherited superiorities. "For according to the standards of our bourgeois world," he writes, "praise or blame pertains to the moral sphere, not to the natural; to praise qualities granted by nature would seem unjust and frivolous to the ordinary man." Here, as elsewhere, the swindler adopts the stately, not to say sententious tone of Goethe's moral generalizations.

In telling of the development of a child into a successful confidence man, Mann was clearly standing the German Bildungsroman on its head. The experiences of boyhood, education, journeys, the influence of friends and teachers, the encounters with a series of women—all these shape Felix' character, as they had Wilhelm Meister's. Doubtless the role assigned to the eternal feminine is the most vulnerable aspect of Goethe's idea of education; Friedrich Schlegel had burlesqued it over a century before Mann did. Felix' experiences are more colorful than Wilhelm's if less edifying. He encounters among others a housemaid named Genovefa, a French blue-stocking, and the Junoesque wife of Professor Kuckuck.

It may be recalled that Wilhelm Meister renounced his theatrical mission and took his place in the practical world. More happy, Felix remains an aesthetic man to the end. He is the antipode of Gustave von Aschenbach: the ultimate comic possibility of the artist type opposed to its tragic extreme. Both *Krull* and *Death in Venice* were conceived in the same year, and actually the rogue is, in Mann's view, closer to the norm than is the ascetic hero. Felix' thefts and similar escapades are motivated less by greed than by the sheer joy of expressing his talent skillfully; essentially he is an artist for art's sake. Rewards are pleasant but non-essential. Felix' mentor Schimmelpreester tells him of the repeated thefts of the sculptor Phidias, arguing a causal relation between genius and criminality. The point of the lesson is not lost. As a boy, Felix plays the violin before a fashionable audience at a West German watering place. His bow has been covered with vaseline so that he does not produce a single audible note, but the audience is enchanted. Here Mann goes a long step beyond his earlier story *The Infant Prodigy*, where the boy pianist is not shamming though many of his audience are. Felix vastly admires acrobats, and remarks that such performers, utterly dedicated to their craft, have ceased to be human. One is described as "a serious angel of recklessness," an apparent echo of Rilke's Fifth Elegy. The word he uses, *Artisten*, means literally acrobats but has an obvious double reference here. One symbolic experience shows Felix the dualistic nature of the representative man, the performer. Taken to an operetta by his father, the boy is entranced

by the elegance, charm, and beauty of the tenor, a singer
with the significantly hyphenated name of Müller-Rosé.
When encountered back stage, divested of rouge and
costume, the tenor is revealed as a vulgar, pimply, re-
pulsively ugly person. Rosé has vanished; only Müller
remains. But Felix is not seriously upset; typically he
draws the optimistic moral that the crassest reality can
be transmuted into beautiful appearance. An ugly insect
may become, at night, a phosphorescent firefly. Felix too
can appear to be what he is not.

Duality of existence, a double life, these are indeed
Krull's central experiences. Mann reminds us, as it were,
of the relation between duplication and duplicity. As
we have seen, Felix leads a double existence in Paris,
and then, in a different sense, while making his grand
tour. Accordingly, he finds the world most to his taste
when the persons he encounters are arranged in pairs:
Doppelbild, a dual image, unity in duality, is one of his
favorite expressions—incidentally another reminiscence
of Goethe's language. In Frankfurt he is entranced by
a handsome brother and sister, apparently twins, and
feels that the beauty of each is enhanced by the other.
(One suspects a mythological or astrological reference
here: Apollo and Diana perhaps, or the Gemini of the
Zodiac.) A pretty girl in Lisbon recalls another in Paris;
Mann, to emphasize that the two are but variations of a
single theme, calls them Zaza and Zouzou. There are
other instances. Felix himself plays the role of Hermes,
the god of thieves, though he has never heard of Hermes
until the blue-stocking in Paris explains his mythical
provenience.

Towards the end of the novel a more serious note is

struck, though never in isolation but polyphonically combined with comedy. Disguised as the Marquis de Venosta, Krull has an astounding conversation with the paleontologist Professor Kuckuck (whose name prevents us from regarding him too solemnly). Despite it, he seems to be a scholar of imagination as well as of erudition. He initiates Felix into the secrets of the universe as they appear to the twentieth-century scientist. When Kuckuck gives him some idea of the incredible dimensions and velocities of the world of post-Einsteinian science, he is enchanted. Above all, Kuckuck gives him a new, expanded sense of time—a theme which here again attracted Mann as it had in *Joseph*. Not only is life, measured by the scale of aeons, a very brief episode:

> . . . *Being itself is one*—[an episode] between Nothingness and Nothingness. Being did not always exist and will not always exist. It had a beginning and will have an end, and then space and time will come to an end too; for they exist only by virtue of Being and are bound together by it.

The latent nihilism of the passage is reinforced by another, a bit later on: "This interdependent whirling and circling, this convolution of gases into heavenly bodies, this burning, flaming, freezing, exploding, pulverizing, this plunging and speeding, bred out of Nothingness and awaking Nothingness—which would perhaps have preferred to remain asleep and was waiting to fall asleep again—all this was Being, known also as Nature, and everywhere in everything it was one." What is a confidence man to make of all this? If one doubts that it would interest him, one should recall that Mann's protagonists have a knack of transcending their usual limitations in moments of enlightenment, just as Hans Castorp did in the snowstorm. Probably it is better to put the question more objectively: what is the relation between the theme of nothingness and the picaresque nature of the story as a whole? The answer, I think, is clear: the purposeless, pointless cosmos, "which would perhaps have preferred to remain asleep," corresponds roughly to the purposeless, amoral society of which a confidence man is the appropriate representative. Death is no longer primarily a matter affecting man; we are confronted by the death of Existence itself. Neither Krull nor his enigmatic mentor is in the least depressed by this prospect. Nor, certainly, is it the intention of the book to depress the reader. *The Confessions of Felix Krull* is a dance on the brink of the abyss, the birth of comedy out of the spirit of nihilism.

One might expect Kuckuck—whose name is one of the euphemisms for the devil—to be cast as a Mephistophelean spirit of denial. The opposite is the case: this time the despair of Prospero is overcome. Precisely because life and existence are impermanent, they command his sympathy. In an essay of 1952, "Praise of Transitoriness," as elsewhere, Mann took a similar position: without the evanescent, fleeting quality of our experience, life would lose its value.

In his words on love, shortly before the end of the book, Felix speaks with a similar sense of sympathy for life. Rather, it is Mann speaking through a mask which has suddenly become transparent:

> Love, Zouzou my love, does not consist simply in the state of being in love where, amazingly, one physically separate body ceases to be unpleasant to another . . . Everywhere in the world there are delicate signs and intimations of its exist-

159

ence. . . . People shake hands—that is something very ordinary, everyday, and conventional; no one thinks anything about it except those who are in love, and they enjoy this contact because as yet no other is allowed them. . . . In truth, however, carefully examined, it belongs in the domain of the miraculous, and it is no small testimonial to Nature's departure from itself, the denial of the aversion of stranger for stranger, a secret sign of omnipresent love.

The late essay on Chekhov (1954) turns significantly on the theme of despair, of the despairing artist. Mann very largely identifies himself with that character in Chekhov's *A Dull Story* who, when challenged by the question "What is to be done?" can give only the disheartened, almost desperate reply: "On my honor, I do not know." Yet in the end the self-doubting, modest artist is justified: his work, his writing, is in itself a moral act.

This interpretation of Chekhov appeared in an East German journal. On first reading, one has the impression that Mann went very far to conciliate the rulers of the so-called "German Democratic Republic"; he speaks, with reference to his own time as well as Chekhov's, of living in a dying society, quotes Lenin, and so on. Actually, however, Mann is "boring from within": the essay is a vindication of the "pure" artist; one does not have to be a "socialist realist," he implies, to be a great and deeply committed writer. Quite subtly, Mann has used Aesopian language to undermine the Communist position. Any East German writer who had published an article with a similar intention would have been fortunate to escape the concentration camp by fleeing to the West; Mann was of course privileged, and made good use of his situation.

The Goethean motif of omnipresent love, briefly sounded in *Krull,* is central in Mann's *Essay on Schiller* (1955) "dedicated in love" to the memory of the great dramatist. This, Mann's last published work, is by far the finest of his critical studies. Highly qualified persons consider it the most admirable interpretation of Schiller ever written. In any case, it is a genuinely creative study: after reading it, one perceives beauties and grandeurs in Schiller's poetry which one had never seen before.

Mann's previous critical portraits had often been esoteric self-portrayals, and this circumstance has annoyed many readers. In the essay on Schiller there is also an autobiographical element; thus Mann makes much of the poet's diligence, and notes that he endeavored to satisfy both the connoisseur and the broad public. This type of identification, however, seems valid in itself; above all it does not divert our attention from Schiller himself. Similarly, Mann's characteristic irony plays only a minor role here; where it does appear, the irony is truly affectionate. Since *Tonio Kröger,* indeed since his boyhood, Mann had often referred to Schiller; at times, as in his fine study *A Weary Hour,* admiration was ambivalently mingled with other emotions. In this last work, enthusiasm has burned away, as it were, the other elements. Schiller appears not only as a great writer but as a hero of the mind, a thinker who could guide mankind away from nationalism "towards art, towards love, towards peace, towards man's salvation in reverence for himself." The master of irony finished his career on a note of affirmation. Like Prospero, whom Mann had quoted out of context when himself depressed, he escaped an ending of despair after all. More fortunate than Shakspere's magician, he was never in want of "art to enchant"; his final work was the crown of his life's achievement.

Mann is too versatile, and above all too individual a writer to be assigned to any school or "-ism." His most representative works, from *Buddenbrooks* on, combine the strains of realism and symbolism, but gradually the latter has become dominant. From this point of view, as from others, *The Magic Mountain* is an apex and a turning point in his development. Employing a microscopic closeness of observation, it adds a new dimension to the realistic novel, while at the same time it marks Mann's major shift to the use of mythical patterns. Yet even in his later, most symbolic works, the accuracy of Mann's eye has not decreased. It would seem that his "dual perspective" on the world—his way of seeing persons and events dialectically, from two sides—gives his vision a stereoptic quality. From this double perspective the extraordinary "realness" of Hans Castorp, say, who is both a "little German bourgeois" and a genius of experience, or of Joseph, scamp and savior, in part derives.

In regarding Mann's literary career, which extended for something over sixty years, one is impressed even more by the sustained quality of Mann's work than by its range. Few novelists, and perhaps no other German novelist, have produced an integrated body of fiction in which the general level is so consistently maintained. If there are few works of the supreme brilliance of *Death in Venice*, there are, with negligible exceptions, none which do not reveal a sense of scrupulous craftsmanship and a fine intellect.

This consistency is doubly remarkable in an *oeuvre*

which includes such contrasts as *Buddenbrooks* and *The Tales of Jacob*, *Little Lizzie* and *Tonio Kröger*, *The Blood of the Walsungs* and *Disorder and Early Sorrow*. It is high time to discard the notion of Mann as a virtuoso performing endless variations on a single theme. The author of "nervous little sketches" and lyrical novellas experienced a rebirth like his own Joseph's before he could produce, in *The Magic Mountain*, one of the most imposing structures erected by the modern mind. The novels and stories of his "third career," from 1933 on, have in turn a character and physiognomy of their own. Some of these later and more experimental works betray a decrease in immediacy and freshness. Yet Mann's last works—the *Confessions of Felix Krull* and the essay on Schiller—are among his most vivid and effective.

In playing his favorite role of mediator between Germany and Europe, artist and bourgeois, the *avant garde* and tradition, Mann has not escaped the general fate of the man in the center: attack from both sides. It would also seem that the somewhat indiscriminate praise heaped upon him in recent years has induced an opposite reaction, as if it were Mann's fault that some dull persons have publicly admired him for the wrong reasons. In any event, such shifts in literary fashion are supremely unimportant. What matters is the totality of Mann's work. It remains a towering and monumental achievement.

BIOGRAPHICAL SKETCH

THOMAS MANN WAS BORN IN LÜBECK ON JUNE 6, 1875. THE
Manns belonged to the "patrician" aristocracy of well-to-
do merchant families which had developed in the North
German Hanseatic cities. Mann's father, Johann Thomas
Heinrich Mann, had risen to the rank of Senator in the
city government; his mother, born Julia Da Silva-Bruhns,
was of partly Brazilian descent. It was a gifted family,
by no means as "decadent" as a reader of *Buddenbrooks*
might infer. Mann's elder brother, Heinrich (1871–1950),
attained a reputation as novelist and essayist which at
times rivaled his own. While the youngest brother, Viktor
(1890–1949), the prototype of Benjamin in *Joseph,* was
less talented, he wrote a long and very readable family
history. Two sisters, Julia and Carla, died in tragic circumstances.

Mann's career as a student at the *Gymnasium* in Lübeck
was neither happy nor particularly distinguished. It is reflected in his account of Hanno Buddenbrook's school-

ing; Heinrich Mann, in his *Small Town Tyrant*, gives a still more acid account of Prussianized education. On the side, Thomas Mann was reading Heine and Schiller, Theodor Storm and the North German humorist Fritz Reuter; and he asserted his individuality by editing, and largely writing, two numbers of a "literary monthly," *Spring Storm*, while still at school.

After the death of Senator Mann in 1891, the family moved to Munich. Thomas remained in Lübeck until 1893, to pursue his studies at the hated *Gymnasium*. In that year, having joined his mother in Munich, he worked briefly for a fire insurance company there, devoting his time in the office to writing his first commercially published story, *Fallen*. After giving up his job, he studied in a rather desultory manner at the University of Munich.

Much more decisive than any academic influences was Mann's first reading, around 1895, of Schopenhauer and Nietzsche. His reaction to the latter was a remarkably discriminating one: "I took nothing literally, I believed almost nothing he said." With his usual good taste, Mann found the doctrines of the Superman and the Blond Beast, like Nietzsche's praise of "Renaissance immoralism," embarrassing. It was Nietzsche the psychologist, the analyst (and exemplar) of decadence, who appealed to him; as did also, one may assume, the philosopher's habit of thinking in gaudy antitheses. Schopenhauer, with his rejection of individuation and his belief in the absolute primacy of will over intellect, Mann took far more literally.

In the mid-Nineties, Mann spent almost a whole year in Italy, staying in Rome and Palestrina with his brother Heinrich. Here he read Scandinavian and Russian novels,

165

avoided German tourists, and began to write *Budden-brooks*. Mann's *Wanderjahre*—if one can apply the term to such a settled young man—are among the most serious and industrious known. At the time, Italy meant little to him as a symbol of Southern beauty; his stay abroad was essentially a chance to test his powers as a writer. When he returned to Munich, he took rooms in Schwabing, then the Greenwich Village of central Europe, and worked for a while as one of the editors of the satirical magazine *Simplicissimus*. Among his colleagues were Jakob Wassermann and the artist and novelist Thomas Theodor Heine. He was also on friendly terms with minor literary figures like Friedrich Huch, Kurt Martens, and Arthur Holitscher, and maintained relations with the "Cosmics," a rather flamboyant sect made up of followers of Stefan George. One of them is preserved in Mann's *At the Prophet's* "like a fly in amber." Neither in his Schwabing days nor later did he become a member of any group or coterie.

Buddenbrooks was completed in Munich. Its publishers, the firm of S. Fischer in Berlin, appalled by the length of the manuscript, had suggested drastic cuts; but Mann stuck to his guns and eventually won his first major success. The novel appeared early in 1901 and, after initial resistance by the German public, became a fabulous best-seller.

In 1905, Mann married Katja Pringsheim. Of their six children, two, Klaus and Erika, were to achieve literary reputations; a third, Golo, became a noted historian. With the possible exception of the Schlegels, the Manns are the most important family in German literary history.

From 1898, when the volume *Little Herr Friedemann* was published, until the outbreak of the First World War, collections of Mann's short stories appeared with some regularity. The most brilliant was *Tristan* (1903); besides the title novella, it included *The Wardrobe, Little Lizzie, Gladius Dei*, and *Tonio Kröger*. The collection *The Infant Prodigy* (1914) is also notable. *Death in Venice* appeared separately in 1912.

A visit to the Lido in 1911 had furnished the raw material for *Death in Venice;* a stay in Davos in 1912 gave the first impulse for writing *The Magic Mountain*. After the First World War, journeys to Italy and to Egypt and the Near East were exploited for *Mario and the Magician* and *Joseph and His Brothers*. Mann has lived quietly, but he has never wasted his experiences; in his artistic economy everything has been subordinated to the demands of production.

The First World War changed Mann from a "non-political" writer to a self-conscious spokesman for Germany. He appeared at first as a romantic conservative, upholding German culture—which then meant to him essentially the spirit of Novalis, Eichendorff, Schopenhauer, Wagner, and Nietzsche—against the "shallow," rationalistic West. By dialectical sleight of hand, he managed to make the arch-rationalist Frederick II of Prussia a symbol of an anti-rationalist Germany. His most "pro-German" and reactionary book, *Reflections of a Non-Political Man* (1918), mirrors a sharp and painful clash with his "Western" brother Heinrich. Although he entered the sphere of politics as an ultraconservative, Mann developed steadily away from his original position. Even

167

in the *Reflections,* the later essays betray the beginning of a shift towards a somewhat rueful acceptance of the coming victory of democracy.

After the German defeat of 1918, Mann turned, in works like *A Man and His Dog* and *Song of the Child,* to the depiction of idyllic domesticity. He soon emerged from this retreat, to play a role as champion of the weak but well-meaning Weimar government. His *The German Republic* (1922) is the work of a romantic who is still a dilettante in politics, dreaming rather pathetically of a synthesis of Novalis and Walt Whitman, Athens and Moscow. Later political addresses, above all his *Appeal to Reason* (1930), a courageous philippic against the Nazis, show a far more responsible facing of political realities. During the same period, Mann became a sort of cultural ambassador to Europe, as his *Account of My Stay in Paris* (*Pariser Rechenschaft,* 1926) and minor pieces bear witness. Three volumes of essays, published between 1922 and 1930, are mainly devoted to literary criticism.

Unlike *Buddenbrooks, The Magic Mountain* (1924) was an immediate success: a German literary historian remarks that the novel taught the nation to read again. Two of Mann's finest novellas, *Disorder and Early Sorrow* (1925) and *Mario and the Magician* (1930), illuminate the mood and the problems of the period between the great wars. Mann's fiftieth birthday, in 1925, was widely celebrated. When he was awarded the Nobel prize in 1929, he was acclaimed, briefly, even in nationalistic circles.

This state of affairs was to change more radically than the most pessimistic had expected. On February 10, 1933,

Mann delivered a lecture, *Suffering and Greatness of Richard Wagner,* to an appreciative Munich audience. (Hitler had become chancellor a few days before but had not yet seized absolute power.) The next day Mann left Germany for a brief trip, as he thought; he was not to return for sixteen years. Warned of the increasing danger, he extended his stay in Switzerland indefinitely. While Mann had no illusions about the nature of the Nazi regime and not the slightest inclination to come to terms with its rulers, he hesitated to denounce it openly, fearing the loss of his German readers. (His literary works were not prohibited in 1933, and the first two volumes of *Joseph and His Brothers* were published in Berlin.) For this hesitation he has been attacked, largely by those who have no conception of what a sacrifice it is for a writer to cut himself off from the public which reads him in his own language. Of course, the uneasy truce between Mann and the German government could not last. Goaded by a provocative article in the *Neue Zürcher Zeitung,* he broke his silence in an open letter published in that newspaper on February 3, 1936. The Nazis proclaimed that he was no longer a German citizen and of course banned his books; the University of Bonn withdrew the honorary doctorate awarded him shortly after the First World War. Mann's reply to the dean of the faculty of philosophy of Bonn is perhaps the finest of his political polemics. In 1937, as a further political gesture, he founded and edited, with Konrad Falke, the magazine *Mass und Wert* ("Measure and Value"). Devoted to the ideals of Mann's "Third Humanism," the journal survived the increasingly inhumane climate of opinion until 1940.

Mann spent over two years at Princeton (1938–41), where he gave lectures on *Faust* and other topics. In the spring of 1941 he moved to Southern California, becoming one of a colony of German and Austrian exiles which included Bruno Walter, Arnold Schönberg, and Franz Werfel. In 1944 he became an American citizen.

His career in this country was extraordinarily active. He found here a new public to replace the one he lost in 1936: *The Magic Mountain* and the great novellas have become part of the standard education of the literate American. His American popularity is a concrete expression of that era of world literature whose coming Goethe foresaw and welcomed. Of Mann's late works, the *Joseph* novels, which appeared in America from 1934 to 1944, have had the greatest success, though they have not equaled either the sales or the renown of *The Magic Mountain*. *The Beloved Returns: Lotte in Weimar* (1940) was well received; his far slighter *The Transposed Heads* (1941) was treated with a rather baffled respect. *Doctor Faustus* (1948) stirred up a lively debate in this country and a bitter controversy—politically oriented in part— in Germany. Of his late novels, *Felix Krull* (1954) proved the most popular, both in this country and abroad. Besides maintaining his literary production, Mann delivered political lectures in many American cities (*The Coming Victory of Democracy* and *This Peace,* published 1938; *This War,* 1940). A series of appeals to the German people, transmitted by the BBC, was only one of many enterprises. Mann's American career stands in ironic contrast to his old belief that the German artist is non-political by definition. In 1949 he returned briefly to Germany to receive a "Goethe prize" in Frankfurt-am-Main, and annoyed some people by proceeding to the Eastern Zone to accept a second Goethe award in Weimar.

In 1952 Mann moved to Kilchberg, near Zürich; his villa there was his home for the remainder of his life, though he did not give up his American citizenship. Residence in neutral Switzerland was appropriate for a mediator between the German cultural tradition and the political liberalism of the West. The United States lost much of its attraction for him after Franklin Roosevelt's death, while to return permanently to Germany was out of the question.

Indeed, his rejection of an appeal—made in an open letter of 1945 by the writer Walter von Molo—to go back to his native land as "a good physician" caused considerable resentment in Germany. Many of his former compatriots also felt, wrongly if understandably, that *Doctor Faustus* was an anti-German book. His views—aesthetic, political, and even religious—were bitterly attacked; his work was occasionally labeled decadent or "merely ironic."

It is pleasant to be able to record that his career nevertheless ended on a note of triumph: both *Felix Krull* and the *Essay on Schiller* were accepted as masterpieces. However belatedly, his German audience came to terms with Thomas Mann. After a year very rich in honors, he died in his Swiss home on August 12th, 1955.

A NOTE ON THE ESSAYS

MANN'S LITERARY ESSAYS ARE REMARKABLY SUBJECTIVE, AND
are crowded with references to his own works and personality. Whether he is dealing with Goethe or Lessing, Wagner or Freud, he tends, consciously or otherwise, to stress
those aspects of his theme which seem to him characteristic of himself. This does not mean that the essays lack
"objective" value, but the note of self-criticism and self-
portraiture is almost as important in them as in Mann's fiction. Broadly regarded, they stand or fall as works of art
rather than, strictly speaking, as criticism. Their finest
passages are generally those of creative or "re-creative"
rather than critical writing: unforgettable descriptions of
Tolstoi on his country estate, of Goethe in his garden at
Weimar, or of Fontane in his old age. Just as Mann's
novels, from *The Magic Mountain* on, contain a great deal
of criticism, some of the essays have a large element of
fiction. *Goethe and Tolstoi* (1922), for example, is an
elaborate musical composition which makes use of the leit-

motif and plays off the heroes of "the spirit," Schiller and Dostoievski, against Goethe and Tolstoi, the "Nature Gods." The essay is an extreme example of Mann's practice, which at times seems almost an obsession, of thinking in antitheses. As Jacques Barzun and others have observed, there is a general lack of sharp, cleanly defined concepts. This fuzziness of terminology seems necessarily related to Mann's habit of "thinking in opposites"; he must occasionally distort his terms to fit them into a neat symmetrical system of polarities.

A cluster of essays surrounds each of the later novels: thus the *Reflections of a Non-Political Man, Experiences of the Occult,* and *Goethe and Tolstoi* illuminate *The Magic Mountain;* the treatments of Freud and Wagner, like several of the papers on Goethe, accompany *Joseph;* and discussions of Nietzsche, Dostoievski, and *Germany and the Germans* are grouped around *Doctor Faustus.* In my brief consideration of some of the more important essays, I have arranged the topics chronologically, according to their apparent importance as factors in Mann's development, and have confined myself to his discussions of figures of international importance.

SCHOPENHAUER, WAGNER, NIETZSCHE

Mann has repeatedly stated that these three romantics formed the constellation which long dominated the intellectual sky of his youth. He has testified to the intensity of his first experience of their works, and especially to the vividness of his "discovery" of Schopenhauer. "Only once does a person read in that way." It is Mann's earlier fiction which best records his reaction to the three figures who

173

stood, in his view, at the very summit of human culture. Rather surprisingly, Mann did not devote an extended essay to any one of them until his influence on him had been greatly modified, though all three play a major part in the *Reflections,* that interminable hymn to German romanticism. In the essays of the Thirties and Forties, Wagner and the two philosophers are considered rather judiciously; the ardor of Mann's first enthusiasm had been lost.

Schopenhauer's basic conviction of the futility of individual activity and volition largely determined the tone of *Buddenbrooks* and of the early stories; his ideal of aesthetic contemplation as an escape from the torments of the will is recalled particularly by *Death in Venice;* his aversion to political activity helped to confirm Mann's patrician conservatism, as the *Reflections* testify. In his long essay on Schopenhauer (1938), Mann gave a sympathetic exposition of his thought. Mann's main intention is to establish "the relation between pessimism and humanism" in Schopenhauer. While his degradation of the intellect to a mere instrument of the will is anti-classical and anti-humanistic, his ethics and his concept of man place him on the side of the "spirit" after all. As one would expect, Mann has come to regard Schopenhauer's "nonpolitical" orientation as petty-bourgeois and philistine.

Mann has always been devoted to Wagner's music, but it is perhaps not too much to say that he feels that the composer's greatest significance is extramusical. In the two long essays devoted to Wagner, he associated his work with that of such "monumental" nineteenth-century

174

writers as Zola, Ibsen, and Tolstoi. Wagner's use of the leitmotif appears as an essentially literary technique, employed primarily to illuminate the psychology of his characters. His music is often subordinated to a dramatic effect; it is anything but "pure." Accordingly, Mann rejects Wagner's "dilettante" concept of the total work of art; he was a great musician and a genuine poet in spite of his theory. Mann regards the "music dramas" largely from the point of view of his own *Joseph* tetralogy, stressing the combination of tremendous scope with attention to detail, and the exploitation of myth and psychology. In Wagner, as in Schopenhauer and Nietzsche, he sees a forerunner of Freud, noting particularly the hysterical figure of Kundry in *Parsifal* and Siegfried's youthful experience of sexual *Angst*. Writing, as so often, with his own position in mind, he emphasizes that Wagner, like Schopenhauer and Goethe, was very much of a burgher. Yet at the same time he was a genius of a particularly questionable sort, a crafty magician whose powerful spells were often sinister, a master of the theatrical and the "daemonic."

Throughout much of his career, Mann belonged to the school which Crane Brinton has called "gentle Nietzscheans"—the interpreters who play down, ignore, or explain away the brutalities of works like *The Will to Power,* while stressing those more civilized aspects of Nietzsche associated with concepts like "the good European." For a long time, Nietzsche seems to have been Mann's greatest intellectual hero. In his rejection of Schopenhauer's pessimism and Wagner's music, Nietzsche was the great conqueror of romanticism, and thus, in a sense, the chief teacher of Hans Castorp. In his works, something "ineffably new" was born. The word "ineffable" of course begs the question, and Mann is vague about the positive direction of Nietzscheanism; he seems to have in mind Nietzsche's belief that "life" is itself the highest of values, and is not to be measured by any extraneous criterion. Yet certainly Mann never accepted the "revaluation of all values," the turn from Christian to Greek standards, which is one of the few tenets which the philosopher consistently upheld. Rather, Mann considered Nietzsche an anti-moralist obsessed with morality, an ascetic, almost a Christian *malgré lui*. Nietzsche often appears as a martyr, indeed as a sort of Christ, who "died a sacrificial death on the cross of thought." The late essay, *Nietzsche's Philosophy in the Light of Contemporary Events* (1947) has a tone of sympathy and not unmixed admiration; it is critical rather than dithyrambic and strongly emphasizes the pathological element in Nietzsche. "The light of contemporary events" has sharply illuminated the "tough" side of Nietzscheanism, and its aftereffects: Nietzsche was egregiously wrong in thinking that "life" was in danger of being overwhelmed by "the spirit"; precisely the opposite is the case. Nietzsche was a complete aesthete, and his work can be accepted only as "an aesthetic phenomenon." The final verdict, drastically reversing Mann's earlier judgment, seems sound. Nietzsche appears less as a prophet or a philosopher than as a master of prose. He is often associated, as an enemy of Western ideas, a brilliant psychologist, and a diseased genius, with Dostoievski.

A NOTE ON THE ESSAYS

After Mann had broken, in the *The Magic Mountain,* with the tradition of Schopenhauer and Wagner, he turned to the search for intellectual heroes of a different stamp, to men who had chosen the side of "life." Nietzsche served for a time, but he was too tragic and perhaps too ambiguous a figure. The greatest of Mann's later heroes was to be Goethe, but he was too complex a figure to be fitted easily into any tradition. Lessing and Freud were invoked earlier than he to lend luster to the cause of the "Third Humanism." The juxtaposition may be startling, but it is not unnatural. Gotthold Ephraim Lessing, the most distinguished critic and dramatist of the German Enlightenment, was an inevitable choice as an exemplar of tolerance, clarity, and rationality. In the Twenties, Mann felt a close affinity to Lessing. The great critic had also been attacked as cold and overintellectual; he too had been labeled a mere "writer," not a genuine poet; he too had been a keen judge of his own work. In demonstrating that Lessing had been a "true German" as well as a cosmopolitan rationalist, a creator as well as a critic, Mann was vindicating himself. In the conclusion of his major essay on Lessing (1929), Mann urged that no true humanistic synthesis could be formed without the element of reason which Lessing typified.

Originally, Freud seems to have appeared to Mann as an heir of the darker tradition of German romanticism, a champion of instinct against reason, the "night side" of existence against light. Between the composition of *The*

Magic Mountain and his first important essay on Freud, *Freud's Position in the History of Modern Thought* (1929), Mann seems to have made his first real study of psychoanalysis. From this time on, Freud is seen as fundamentally a rationalist, as a great explorer investigating the subconscious for the sake of the conscious. The Ego is delicate and weak—it is the Hans Castorp of the psyche—and Freud, as a man of good will, wishes to help it against the mighty Id.

Like the essay on Lessing, Mann's interpretation of Freud must be read in the context of the times. It too has a polemical element, directed against the Nazis in particular and German "irrationalism" in general. (By irrationalism Mann means the powerful movement in German thought which proclaimed the inferiority of the intellect to the will, the subconscious, instinct, or "the blood.") The irrationalists are fundamentally right, Mann holds, in declaring reason the weaker party; but eternally wrong if, like Naphta, they glory in the frailty of the intellect and try completely to destroy its already precarious control. The great value of Freudian psychology, to Mann, is that it combines a highly "modern" knowledge of the depths of the psyche with the humane and fundamentally rational goal of replacing darkness by light, Id by Ego. Throughout the essay, it is apparent that Mann is engaging in cultural propaganda, and making a gallant effort to persuade his German public that it is possible to be both decent and "deep," both reasonable and modern.

While *Freud and the Future* (1936) restates the major points of the earlier essay, it is largely concerned with the relations between literature and psychoanalysis, both of which conceive of disease as an instrument of knowledge. Although it was first delivered as a speech in honor of Freud's eightieth birthday, it is extremely autobiographical and self-conscious. Mann devoted a great deal of attention to his own use of psychoanalytic insights in *Joseph,* and stressed that many of Freud's ideas had been anticipated by Novalis, Schopenhauer, Kierkegaard, and Nietzsche. This apparently tactless address may well have annoyed many of the faithful who had gathered for the celebration in Vienna, but Freud himself—for whom Mann gave a personal reading—was delighted by it. In the eulogistic sections of the speech, Mann emphasized that psychoanalysis had revolutionized the most varied studies, and maintained that Freud's lifework would be used as a cornerstone in building a new humanity. He rightly pointed to Freud's high rank as a writer and his intellectual courage. Through the courage to be pessimistically realistic, Freud is associated with Schopenhauer, with Dürer's knight who defied "death and the devil," and ultimately with the defiant figure of Lessing.

GOETHE

Mann's relation to Goethe has gone through a long evolution. Until the early Twenties, he seems to have been far more attracted by more "modern" figures like Wagner and Nietzsche. Even in *Goethe and Tolstoi,* the German poet is less vividly drawn than the Russian novelist, who is seen as a mythic figure, a "Russian god under a golden lime tree." Mann's comparative method, in this essay, leads him to stress and overstress the resemblances between the two writers, who both appear godlike, "close to nature" (in Schiller's sense), and relatively healthy, though each has a negative, nihilistic side. Goethe, the more dignified, civilized figure, seems a bit pale and stiff beside the vigorous animality of Tolstoi.

The two essays evoked by the centennial of Goethe's death in 1932, *Goethe's Career as a Man of Letters* and *Goethe as a Representative of the Bourgeois Age*, show striking changes. As the titles imply, Mann has begun to associate himself more and more closely with the poet. (He has never posed as Goethe reborn, but claims "a certain family resemblance.") Among other points, he emphasizes that Goethe was a burgher with a sound sense for business, a master of prose style as well as a poet, a realist, an inveterate educator; a profoundly ironical "double-souled nature," yet a great reconciler of antitheses. No patriot, he was thoroughly German. All of these positions are well taken; that the poet who appears in these essays resembles Thomas Mann nearly as much as Goethe is the result of a process of emphasis and selection which was presumably largely unconscious. There was also a didactic motive for presenting Goethe as a "steady-going poet." Writing at a time when the Germans were turning more and more to a cult of irrationality, Mann confronted his countrymen with a reasonable, civilized figure rather than the wild young genius of the Storm and Stress.

In recent years, Mann's image of Goethe has again changed. In such essays as his *Phantasy on Goethe* (1948), the poet appears as the ideal German, combining the rude vigor of Luther with the urbane culture of Erasmus; Germanic energy with Mediterranean civilization. In a still broader reference, he becomes the paradigm of Man, the bearer of the double blessing. The *Phantasy* consists largely of a highly condensed sketch of Goethe's whole career. Despite his ambivalences and his "nihilism," he was fundamentally "friendly to life." By concluding the essay with Goethe's line, "The only thing that counts in the end is progress," Mann gives an added emphasis to his belief, often stated earlier, that Goethe was one of the great liberators of the human spirit.

Paradoxically, the characterization of Goethe in *Lotte in Weimar* is more satisfying and "objective" than that of the essays. In the novel Mann was primarily concerned with giving a total picture rather than establishing a particular thesis. Two of Mann's less ambitious Goethe papers, on *Faust* (1938) and *Werther* (1941), are excellent: they are focused on the works themselves. Several of the late essays are important; the admirable interpretations of Chekhov (1954) and Schiller (1955) are discussed above, at the end of Chapter 8.

NOTES

(Books and articles not identified in detail here are more fully described in the bibliography.)

PAGE

5   *Peeperkorn and Tolstoi:* see André von Gronicka, "Thomas Mann and Russia.'

8   *Lombroso:* While his most important book appeared in 1864, its impact did not strike Germany until considerably later.

13   *Heine and Theodor Storm:* compare also Mann's three youthful poems "Repeated Farewell," "You see, my child, I love you," and "Monologue." They have not been translated into English.

26   *Here two forces* . . . Lowe-Porter translation; in *Stories of Three Decades* (New York: Knopf, 1936), p. 153.

31   *T. S. Eliot:* in *The Use of Poetry and the Use of Criticism* (London, 1933), p. 156.

35   *"He had himself sprung . . .":* H. H. Boyesen in the preface to Kielland's *Tales of Two Countries* (New York, 189'), p. xii.

37   *André von Gronicka:* in "Thomas Mann and Russia."

38   *The testimony of his brother:* see Viktor Mann, *Wir Waren Fünf.*

NOTES

PAGE

41f. *Have I hoped to live on* . . . Lowe-Porter translation; in
      Buddenbrooks (New York: Knopf, 1946), p. 527.

46f. *Soft and clear as a bell* . . . Lowe-Porter translation, *ibid.*,
      p. 413.

63   *Vernon Venable:* in "Poetic Reason in Thomas Mann."

68   *the world about him was out of joint:* see Georg Lukacs,
      Thomas Mann (Berlin, 1949), p. 39f.

72   *devoting almost a quarter:* see H. J. Weigand, *Thomas Mann's
      Novel "Der Zauberberg,"* p. 15.

73   *amalgam of ideas and phrases:* see Weigand, p. 10ff., 162ff.

75   *As has been remarked:* by Johanna Graefe, *Über den Zauber-
      berg von Thomas Mann* (Berlin, 1947), p. 35f.

78   *the trauma inflicted by hideous experiences:* pointed out by
      Mr. Harry Slochower in a lecture given March 18, 1950.

81   *parallels the development of Germany:* see Weigand, pp. 96–
      139.

83   *a sort of Christ:* see J. C. Thirlwall, "Orphic Influences in
      The Magic Mountain," *Germanic Review,* XXV (1950), 290–
      298.

85   *"The Great Stupor"* and *"The Great Irritation":* in Mrs. Lowe-
      Porter's translation these chapter titles are given as "The Great
      God Dumps" and "Hysterica Passio."

85   *charge of infamy:* an echo of Heinrich Mann's attack on
      his brother's political position during the First World
      War.

88   *autobiographical account:* still another one is Mann's *Song of
      Childhood* (1919), a sort of domestic epic written in rather
      prosaic hexameters.

89   *city of political adventurers:* see Peter Viereck, *Metapolitics,*
      New York, 1941.

90   *implications about the* . . . *artist:* on this point my essay
      about *Mario* in *The Stature of Thomas Mann,* pp. 168–173,
      should be corrected.

92   *"the most powerful hypnotist* . . ." and *"long-toothed Anglo-
      Saxoness":* Lowe-Porter translation, *Stories of Three Decades,*
      pp. 556, 561.

183

98 *to show typical and timeless figures:* see Hamburger, *Thomas Manns Roman "Joseph und seine Brüder,"* pp. 31–34.

99 *to expand his old technique:* see Peter Heller, "Some Functions of the Leitmotiv in Thomas Mann's Joseph Tetralogy," *Germanic Review,* XXII (1947), 126–141.

105 *Osiris, to whose role he . . . adapts himself:* see Kerényi, *Romandichtung und Mythologie,* p. 30.

106 *Osiris among the reeds:* Isis hid the infant Osiris (or Horus) in the bulrushes. See W. Max Müller, in *A Mythology of All Races,* XII (*Egyptian*), p. 116. The anticipation of the story of Moses must have fascinated Mann, as his *The Tables of the Law* indicates.

107 *highly qualified critic:* H. J. Weigand in *Monatshefte für deutschen Unterricht,* XXIX (1937), 241–256.

107 *Schepses-Bes:* Bes was an Egyptian dwarf-god. See Müller, p. 61ff.

108 *that Potiphar was a eunuch:* see Hamburger, pp. 72, 155.

108 *ambivalent goddess:* in some versions of the myth Ishtar causes the death of Tammuz, her lover and son. See *A Mythology of All Races,* V (*Semitic*) by S. H. Langdon, p. 28.

111 *the historical Amenhotep IV:* Egyptologists are divided on the extent of his final accomplishment. See James Baikie, *A History of Egypt,* II (New York and London, 1929), pp. 227–379. In an article in *Imago,* I (1912), which Mann may well have read, Karl Abraham maintained that Amenhotep was a neurotic.

112 *Amarna "Hymns to Aton":* the translation is by Aylward Blackman, based on the German version of A. Erman. Quoted in Baikie, II, 375–78.

113 *Franklin Roosevelt:* Mann's vast admiration for him is explicitly stated in *Die Entstehung des Doktor Faustus.*

114 *"artist as leader":* see William Troy, "Thomas Mann: Myth and Reason."

115 *Willa Cather:* in *Not over Forty,* p. 121f.

118 *task of commentator:* see Hamburger, pp. 31–34.

119 *decrease in intensity:* Harry Levin makes this point about

NOTES

Joseph the Provider specifically. See *The Stature of Thomas Mann*, p. 214.

123   *concentric circles:* see Ernst Cassirer, "Thomas Manns Goethe-Bild."

126   *Hindu legend:* the famous Indologist Heinrich Zimmer suggested the subject to Mann.

132   *the author himself might have become:* see H. A. Maier in *Modern Language Quarterly*, IX (1948), 343–353.

137   *The Germans have . . .* Lowe-Porter translation, *Doctor Faustus*, p. 84.

138   *Victor Oswald:* in "Thomas Mann's *Doktor Faustus:* The Enigma of Frau von Tolna."

139   *image of the loom: Faust*, 11. 1924–27. Taylor translation.

140   *. . . grant that expressiveness . . .* Lowe-Porter translation. *Doctor Faustus*, p. 491.

144   *"secret identity": Die Entstehung des Doktor Faustus*, p. 82.

151   *"quite uncertain":* Lowe-Porter translation, *The Holy Sinner*, p. 10.

159   *"This interdependent":* Lindley translation, *Krull*, p. 274.

160   *"Love, Zouzou":* ibid., p. 364 f.

165   *family history: Wir Waren Fünf.*

170   *had no illusions . . . about the Nazi regime:* see his *Leiden an Deutschland* (Los Angeles, 1944), which contains sections of Mann's diary of 1933–1934.

174   *Jacques Barzun:* in the *Nation*, CLVII, 1 (July 3, 1948), p. 20 f.

179   *his first real study of psychoanalysis:* see W. F. Michael in *Modern Language Notes*, LXV (1950), 165–171.

180   *Mann's relation to Goethe:* see Bernhard Blume, *Thomas Mann und Goethe*, Bern, 1949.

180   *"Freud himself":* see Mann's unpublished letter to H. Hatfield, May, 1951.

181   *"steady-going poet":* Lowe-Porter translation, *Essays of Three Decades*, p. 70.

BIBLIOGRAPHY

SINCE THIS BRIEF BIBLIOGRAPHY OF THOMAS MANN'S WORKS has been prepared with the American reader in mind, I have concentrated on translations published in the United States. It makes no claim to completeness. (Of the several available editions of Mann's collected works in German, the *Gesammelte Werke* [Frankfurt a. M., 1960] in twelve volumes is the most satisfactory as well as the most recent.) The secondary "literature" about Mann is enormous; I have tried merely to list a few books and articles which seem especially important. Except for a few particularly relevant works in German, I have excluded all material not available in English.

The two most important bibliographies supplement each other admirably. Hans Bürgin's *Das Werk Thomas Manns* (Frankfurt a. M., 1959) is the standard listing of all Mann's writings, in the original and in translation; it includes even the titles of his few known drawings and of the various phonograph recordings of parts of his work. In contrast, *Fifty Years of Thomas Mann Studies* by

BIBLIOGRAPHY

Klaus W. Jonas (Minneapolis, 1955) is mainly devoted to books and articles about Mann.

The dates given for Mann's works in my text naturally refer to the German originals; those listed below, to the time of American publication. Unless the bibliography states otherwise, the translator of all works listed in sections 1–3 is Mrs. H. T. Lowe-Porter and the publisher is Alfred A. Knopf, New York.

THOMAS MANN

LONGER NARRATIVES

Royal Highness. Translated by A. Cecil Curtis. 1916.

Buddenbrooks. 1924.

The Magic Mountain. 1927.
> The first volume of the Joseph tetralogy, *Die Geschichten Jaakobs,* appeared under the misleading title of *Joseph and His Brothers* in 1934.

Young Joseph. 1935.

Joseph in Egypt. 1938.

Joseph the Provider. 1944.

Joseph and His Brothers. (A one-volume edition of the entire tetralogy.) 1948.

The Beloved Returns: Lotte in Weimar. 1940.

The Transposed Heads. 1941.

Doctor Faustus. 1948.

The Holy Sinner. 1951.

The Black Swan. Translated by W. R. Trask. 1954.

Confessions of Felix Krull, Confidence Man. Translated by Denver Lindley. 1955.

COLLECTIONS OF STORIES

Death in Venice and Other Stories. Translated by Kenneth Burke. 1925.

Children and Fools. Translated by H. G. Scheffauer. 1928.

Stories of Three Decades. 1936. The standard American collection. Three early stories, *Fallen, Death,* and *The Will to Happiness,* are excluded. *The Tables of the Law* appeared first in an anthology, *The Ten Commandments* (Simon and Schuster, 1944) in a translation by George R. Marek; then in a new translation by Mrs. Lowe-Porter, 1945.

COLLECTIONS OF ESSAYS AND POLITICAL ADDRESSES

Three Essays. 1929. On Goethe and Tolstoi; Frederick the Great; and "An Experience in the Occult."

Past Masters and Other Papers. 1933. Thirteen essays.

Freud, Goethe, Wagner. 1937. Translated by H. T. Lowe-Porter and Rita Matthias-Reil.

Order of the Day. 1942. Political essays and speeches. Translated by H. T. Lowe-Porter, Eric Sutton, and Agnes E. Meyer.

Listen, Germany! Twenty-five radio messages. 1943.

Essays of Three Decades. 1947. The most inclusive and important collection.

Last Essays. Translated by Richard and Clara Winston and Tania and James Stern. 1959.

SOME UNCOLLECTED ESSAYS

A Sketch of My Life. New York, 1960.

The Problem of Freedom. New Brunswick, N.J., 1939.

The Theme of the Joseph Novels. Washington, 1943.

"What is German?" *Atlantic Monthly,* CLXXIII (May, 1944), 78–85.

Germany and the Germans. Washington, 1945.

"The Years of My Life." *Harper's Magazine,* CCI (1950), 250–264.

OTHER ITEMS

Letters to Paul Amann, 1915–1952. Translated by Richard and Clara Winston. Middletown, Conn., 1960.

The Story of a Novel. Translated by Richard and Clara Winston. New York, 1961.

BIBLIOGRAPHY

SECONDARY STUDIES

BOOKS

Eloesser, Arthur. *Thomas Mann: Sein Leben und seine Werke.* Berlin, 1925.
> Contains valuable biographical data.

Hamburger, Käte. *Thomas Manns Roman "Joseph und seine Brüder."* Stockholm, 1945.

Heller, Erich. *The Ironic German: a Study of Thomas Mann.* Boston, 1958.

Hoffman, Frederick J. *Freudianism and the Literary Mind.* Baton Rouge, La., 1945.
> Remarks on Mann: pp. 209–229.

Kaufmann, Fritz. *Thomas Mann; the World as Will and Representation.* Boston, 1957.

Kerényi, Karl, ed. *Romandichtung und Mythologie: ein Briefwechsel mit Thomas Mann.* Zürich, 1945.
> His correspondence with Mann, largely on mythological matters.

——— *Gespräch in Briefen.* Zürich, 1960.
> A greatly enlarged edition of the above item.

Lindsay, J. M. *Thomas Mann.* Oxford, 1954.

Mann, Erika. *The Last Year: a Memoir of my Father.* Translated by Richard Graves. London, 1958.

Mann, Monika. *Past and Present.* Translated by F. F. Reid and Ruth Hein. New York, 1960.

Mann, Viktor. *Wir Waren Fünf: Bildnis der Familie Mann.* Konstanz, 1949.
> A large-scale, genial family portrait, by Mann's younger brother.

Neider, Charles, ed. *The Stature of Thomas Mann.* New York, 1947.
> A long anthology of eulogy and criticism; contains some valuable pieces not easily found elsewhere. Cited below as "Neider."

Thomas, R. H. *Thomas Mann: the Mediation of Art.* Oxford, 1956.

Weigand, Hermann J. *Thomas Mann's Novel "Der Zauberberg."* New York, 1933.

> The best commentary on *The Magic Mountain.*

ARTICLES

Blackmur, R. P. "Hans Castorp, Small Lord of Counterpositions." *Hudson Review*, I (1948), 318–339.

Burkhard, Arthur. "Thomas Mann's Treatment of the Marked Man." *PMLA*, XLIII (1928), 561–568.

Cassirer, Ernst. "Thomas Manns Goethe-Bild: Eine Studie über Lotte in Weimar." *Germanic Review*, XX (1945), 166–194.

> The best essay on *The Beloved Returns;* should be translated.

Cather, Willa. "Joseph and His Brothers." In *Not Under Forty* (New York, 1936), pp. 96–122.

Du Bos, Charles. "Homage to Thomas Mann." Translated by W. M. Frohock. *Germanic Review*, XXV (1950), 275–284.

> Makes suggestive comparisons with Henry James and Barrès.

Enright, D. J. "The Forgotten Novelist: A Survey of Thomas Mann." In *Focus II* (1946), 104–116.

Frank, Joseph. "Reaction as Progress: or, The Devil's Domain." *Hudson Review*, II (1949), 38–53.

> On *Doctor Faustus.*

Gronicka, André von. "Thomas Mann and Russia." *Germanic Review*, XX (1945), 105–137. Reprinted, in abbreviated form, in Neider, pp. 307–325.

Levin, Harry. "Joseph the Provider." Neider, pp. 211–217.

Lukacs, Georg. "In Search of the Bourgeois." Neider, pp. 469–473.

Neider, Charles. "The Artist as Bourgeois." Neider, pp. 330–357.

Oswald, Victor A., Jr. "Thomas Mann's *Doktor Faustus:* The Enigma of Frau von Tolna." *Germanic Review*, XXIII (1948), 249–253.

Phillips, William. "Thomas Mann: Humanism in Exile." *Partisan Review*, IV (1938), 3–10.

BIBLIOGRAPHY

Rice, Philip Blair. "The Merging Parallels: Mann's *Doctor Faustus*."
  Kenyon Review, XI (1949), 199–217.

Stein, J. M. "Adrian Leverkühn as a Composer." *Germanic Review*, XXV (1950), 257–274.

Troy, William. "Thomas Mann: Myth and Reason." *Partisan Review*, V (1938), 24–32; 51–64.

Venable, Vernon. "Poetic Reason in Thomas Mann." *Virginia Quarterly Review*, XIV (1938), 61–76. In Neider, pp. 129–141, as "Death in Venice."

Weigand, Hermann J. "Thomas Mann's Gregorius." *Germanic Review*, XXVII (1952), 10–30; 83–93.

Wilkinson, E. M. "Aesthetic Excursus on Thomas Mann's *Akribie*." *Germanic Review*, XXXI (1956), 225–235.

INDEX

192

INDEX

INDEX

195